Back to Your Roots:
How to Grow Vegetables & Fruits

Back to Your Roots:
How to Grow Vegetables & Fruits

Patrick DeRojas

"Farmer Pat"

First Printing: 2019

ISBN 978-1-7332095-0-2

Amazon Print ISBN 978-1-6715880-2-8

eBook ISBN 978-1-7332095-1-9

www.farmerpat.net

YouTube – Farmer Pat. Back to Your Roots
Instagram – farmer_pat_youtube
Facebook – farmer pat @produceyourproduce
Gmail – farmerpat240@gmail.com

In Memory of Rayford Petroski

Contents

Acknowledgements

"A truly good book teaches me better than to read it. I must soon lay it down and commence living on its hint. What I began by reading, I must finish by acting."

Henry David Thoreau

Thanks to my family, friends, mentors, and educators.

Disclaimer

The content in this book is designed to offer information on the subjects discussed. The following information is meant for educational purposes only. This book is sold with the agreement that the author and publisher are not offering medical advice of any kind, nor is this book meant to replace medical advice, nor to diagnose, prescribe, or treat any disease, condition, illness, or injury. For diagnosis or treatment of any medical problem, consult a licensed medical physician. It is imperative before starting any diet, lifestyle, or exercise program, that you obtain medical approval from a licensed physician. Author and publisher claim no responsibility to any person or entity for any liability, loss, or damage caused or alleged to be caused directly or indirectly as a result of the use, application, or interpretation of the material in this book.

Introduction

Whether you are driving down Main Street in a small town or walking around a busy city, it is increasingly obvious that more and more people are physically and mentally out of shape. While specialists of all kinds are trying to determine the causes and remedies to these problems, could it be that the answer is very basic and has been in front of us the whole time? The solution to combating increasing rates of obesity, diabetes, heart disease, cancer and other physical diseases, can also alleviate the various mental problems many of us feel. In addition, this lifestyle can improve our self-esteem and our relationships with one another. Besides improving our health, this resolution can enhance the health of the earth by lowering pollution.

The answer I am talking about is for people to start growing their own food! With a welcoming embrace, nature will physically and mentally nurture anybody who gets back to their roots, back to growing vegetables and fruits. Amazingly, a study in Japan indicated when people spent just twenty minutes walking in and looking at nature, they experienced a 13.4% reduction in Salivary Cortisol, which is an indicator of overall stress.[1] Within three days of being exposed to nature, the studies' participants displayed a 50% increase in Natural Killer Cells.[1] This is extremely beneficial for our health, since these white blood cells (lymphocytes) are capable of combating various pathogens, cancers, infections and have the ability to regulate blood sugar levels.[2] Overall, a reduction in sympathetic nerve activity, or the body's response to stress and threats ("fight or flight") was experienced.[1] As a result, cortisol, blood pressure and pulse rates were reduced. Simultaneously, parasympathetic nerve activity increased. This helps to improve our health by relaxing the body, lowering our heart rate, and increasing gland and digestion activity.[1]

Better than merely being a short-term observer of nature, better than just going for a hike to take a selfie atop the mountain, is to become an active lifelong participant in nature through activities like growing food. If you are already awed and inspired by your time in nature, imagine how much more connected you will feel when you actually know how to live from the land. Learning how to grow food will satisfy your stomach and your spirit. When you finally eat food you grew yourself, it will fill you with a sense of gratitude and happiness unbeknownst to your current self. Throughout each season, you will not have to wonder who you are or what to do, since nature will provide the reason and the rhyme for the rest of time. In addition to an enhanced sense of connection to life and more powerful purpose, you will be healthier since you will be eating more homegrown fruits and vegetables. Moreover, after the initial cost of establishing a garden, you will save countless amounts of money by growing your own food. A wise saying is that for every $20 dollars you spend on your garden, you save $200 dollars at the grocery store. Because you will be healthier, you will spend significantly less money on health-care costs throughout life.

What has taken me a lifetime of experience and learning from trial and error, obtaining a Bachelor's of Science in Agriculture at The Pennsylvania State University and the guidance of numerous mentors, I have condensed into an easy to understand yet thorough book. Furthermore, after explaining how to grow fruits and vegetables, I have included a "Health Benefits" section. By using multiple sources of peer reviewed scientific studies, I indicate how the various polyphenols, or the plant chemicals responsible for the color of the fruits and vegetables (a.k.a. anti-oxidants), can improve your health. For instance, these anti-oxidants help prevent a wide variety of diseases, including: heart disease (atherosclerosis), cancer, diabetes, dementia, macular degeneration, stroke, etc. As the ancient Greek Hippocrates said, "Your medicine is your food and your food your medicine." When I was trying to determine what major to study in college, multiple people told me to follow the family footsteps and study medicine since there are numerous jobs available in healthcare. I wondered why so many people are sick in the first place? Ultimately, I decided it was wiser to influence people to change their lifestyle by growing food and becoming more active in nature. The more people we can influence to grow food, the less people will get sick.

Besides the health benefits of consuming these homegrown fruits and vegetables, the physical actions of working outside in the sunshine and soil will significantly improve your health. For example, when you are working in the garden and your hands are exposed to beneficial soil bacteria such as *M. vaccae*, an increase in serotonin levels takes place.[2] Serotonin production is important because it affects numerous aspects of life such as: improving appetite, behavior, digestion, memory, sleep, and sexual performance.[2] Furthermore, consider how exposure to sunlight while growing food will enhance your health. There are hundreds of genes that are activated by sunlight and production of vitamin-D, which have a major influence on our mental and physical well being.[2] Specifically, sunshine influences the gene pro-opiomelanocortin (POMC).[2] This releases opioid peptides that cause us to feel warm and happy, while simultaneously helping to protect our skin against melanoma.[2] In addition, sunlight triggers the gene PTPN2, helping to prevent type 1 diabetes, Crohn's disease, and numerous autoimmune diseases.[3] Also, sunlight activates the BGLAP gene, which strengthens our skeletal structure by making osteocalcin.[2] How many doctors tell their patients that perhaps instead of a pill for their disease, that they need more exposure to the soil and sunshine? As an alternative to having to self-medicate with prescribed and or illegal drugs, alcohol and other excessive behaviors, time in the garden with sunshine on our shoulders and soil on our hands can help us feel better.

Moreover, the physical act of growing food is a natural form of exercise which will help keep you mentally and physically healthy. Modern exercise science reveals to get the most results from working out, it is important to vary our exercise routines. Luckily, if you begin growing food, nature naturally does this. For example, the physical work one does in the garden is always changing throughout the seasons. From putting up fencing around your garden, tilling the soil, pushing the wheelbarrow, etc, you will constantly have a new physical reason for each season. Just like when we exercise, the manual labor performed in the garden will have positive effects on our health. Specifically, as you are doing physical work around the garden, your heart rate will increase and release neurotransmitters such as gamma-aminobutyric acid (GABA) and dopamine.[2] These neurotransmitters will relax your nervous system while improving your mood.[2] If you are experiencing anxiety and depression, you can potentially have low GABA levels.[2] Luckily, one of the ways this can potentially be reversed is by the physical requirements of growing food. Additionally, exercise promotes higher levels of brain derived neurotrophic factor (BDNF).[4] This enhances learning and mental performance because of an increase in neuron production and brain plasticity.[4] Overall, this causes the brain to create new connections and memories which will help the brain continue to function efficiently, especially later in life.[4] Therefore, if science reveals how physical exercise improves our mental and physical health, regular physical exertion outside in the garden will have similar effects.

Furthermore, growing food and working outside will help you to concentrate better. Did you ever notice how your mind settles down and you feel calm after performing manual labor like shoveling snow or raking leaves? While you are doing manual labor, eventually you think less because the task is repetitive. All of a sudden, you are no longer worrying about what you have to do tomorrow, but rather you find yourself in the moment, feeling the wind grace your face and the sunshine smile upon your soul. Simultaneously, since you are also "exercising", the release of neurotransmitters like GABA and dopamine will help you relax and feel good. Unfortunately, too often people want to take the easy way out and have a quick fix such as taking a pill to help them focus.

For instance, according to the Centers for Disease Control from 2003 to 2011, Attention Deficit Hyperactivity Disorder (ADHD) diagnosis increased 42%.[5] From 2007 to 2011, prevalence of medicated ADHD increased by 28%.[5] Perhaps their "disorder" would become order if they spent more time being a participant in nature. If people (especially kids) had to go outside to do some chores on a regular basis, this might help them get rid of excess energy and teach them how to relax and focus. Moreover, they may behave and feel better if instead of eating processed foods high in sugar and preservatives, they ate a natural and whole food-based diet they helped to grow.

Besides helping us to focus better, the act of growing, harvesting, cooking and eating a meal together will strengthen a family's bond. Consider the behavior of families since the dawn of time. In order to survive, they had no choice but to get along, to forgive one another and to become the best of friends. Could the fact that most families no longer work as a team to live from the land be one of the reasons why the family unit is not as strong as it once was? Currently, there are numerous couples and families sitting next to one another in the office of a therapist or family counselor. How many specialists are telling their patients that part of their healing should be getting back to being participants in nature? How many times when the kids said "thank you for dinner" or when the family said "grace" before the meal (if they even say thanks or grace) was it sincere? If we got back to living together as one with the land the way families did since the dawn of time, we would be happier and healthier as a family.

In addition, growing food will significantly improve the health of the environment by reducing the amount of resources needed to maintain our lives. The average American meal now travels about 1500 miles from farm to table.[6] Imagine how fewer resources would be used if instead your meal traveled fifteen feet to the table! Your food will not have to be grown using excessive amounts of fertilizers and sprays. If you are concerned about being exposed to toxins from sprays in your food, you have more control over this issue if you grow food yourself. Also, your food will not have to be wrapped in plastic, cardboard and various packaging and then shipped around the world to the grocery store. Now, you will not have to drive to the grocery store to buy food that is taken home in plastic bags. Instead, you can pick your fruits and vegetables fresh and carry them into the kitchen with your hands or with a reusable item like a wooden basket. Then you can store this food in sustainable items like glass jars which can be reused year after year. Even if you are supplementing part of your diet with homegrown food, the impact on your health and the health of the planet will be significant.

I have often noticed that people who participate in nature for the acquisition of their food seldom throw food away, because they appreciate and understand the source of the food. Unfortunately, according to The United Nations Environment Program and World Resources Institute, approximately 1/3 of all food produced in the world is wasted.[7] With a rapidly increasing population and a dwindling supply of natural resources, this is ignorant and unsustainable. How many times when you eat, do you throw food away? If more of us grew food, this would reduce the amount of food and resources wasted because we would be less likely to discard homegrown food.

Throughout the world, countless people are worried about environmental destruction. Often, you hear them point the blame at others such as politicians, climate treaties, etc. Yet I have a simple question for these environmental advocates; do you grow your own food? Ultimately, if we are concerned about the health of the planet, then we must not look to others to solve these problems, but rather we must be the solution! Whether you live in the country, the suburbs, or the cities, growing food is one of the best ways to improve the health of the earth. People in the cities must begin to install more rooftop and community gardens. Throughout cities, there are countless abandoned lots which can be transformed into community gardens. This can be a wonderful opportunity for people to come together and to have more access to healthier food. Additionally, in the suburbs, there is plenty of space in front and backyards for people to install vegetable gardens and plant fruit trees. How much more beautiful would your neighborhood be if instead of competing with your neighbors over who has nicer grass, you helped one another grow food? Consider how pleasant it would be to have extra produce, that without hesitation, you could share with your neighbors, friends and family. Out in the countryside, more people must get back to growing food. There are too many unused farms in need of restoration so they can become a functioning farm again. These old farms brought back to life can provide abundant harvests, possible income, generate jobs and restore community values.

With a rising population and a substantial distance from farm to table, we must ask ourselves, could we survive if our area was cut off from the food supply? A few generations ago, most people could answer yes to that question. Though we live in a time of material abundance and are producing more food than ever before, our society is becoming more unstable. We are foolish for placing our survival entirely on other people to grow and ship the food we eat hundreds and thousands of miles to our stores and homes. While driving around your neighborhood (which was probably built on old farmland), notice how few gardens are in people's yards. How many farms are still producing food in your area? If in large numbers, more people began to grow food in the city, suburbs and countryside, if more people preserved the food they grew and kept a loaded pantry, we can avoid future disruptions in the food supply. Just look at how Hurricane Maria (2017) which devastated Puerto Rico caused severe food shortages. Imagine if such a disruption occurred on a wide scale level and there was a massive, long-term food shortage in your city, town, state and country.

Let us be remembered as the generation that used our incredible technology to save one another and the earth. If we do not rapidly change our lifestyles, then we will experience many unfortunate consequences. We will see increasing rates of physical and mental diseases, the continued decline of the family and community, violent hostilities over inevitable disruptions in the food supply and ultimately the destruction of the earth. Luckily, the act of growing food, regardless of your gender, race, religion, profession, or personal beliefs, can unite humanity and significantly reduce pollution. If you want to live a happier and healthier life, while improving the health of the earth, then it is time for you to start growing food. Luckily for you, I have condensed this information so you can easily learn how to grow food in a short amount of time, yet the benefits of growing your own food will be with you for the rest of time.

Chapter 1: Preparing Before Planting

Before planting fruits and vegetables, it is essential to amend and improve the soil. Preparing ahead in the months and year(s) prior to planting your garden, will increase yields and make your experience more enjoyable. If you decide to plant a garden anywhere without much consideration, chances are you will encounter problems. This will potentially deter you from future attempts at this healthy lifestyle. You will experience more success and satisfaction growing your own food, if you take the time and effort to understand the following concepts and implement these essential procedures before planting.

Site Selection

The first step for a successful and enjoyable garden is selecting a suitable site. Of utmost importance, make sure the garden receives a minimum of six or more hours of full, direct sunlight per day. While other conditions such as the soil structure can be improved, there is not much you can do if you plant a garden in a shady spot. Of course, you can cut down some trees but why do extra work if it can be avoided? Regarding trees, choose a garden site far away from large trees, which can compete for sun, water, and nutrients. Interestingly, a tree's root system usually extends to underneath the outermost branches (drip line) and sometimes beyond. Another way to check if you are a safe distance away from a tree is to pretend the tree fell down. Is your garden outside of that drop zone? If so, then your garden should be a safe distance away from the tree and should not have any interference from the tree's roots. Luckily, if you have limited options and there are trees close by to where you want to plant your garden, you can avoid tree-root interference by planting in raised beds.

One tree which you definitely want to avoid having near a garden is walnut (keep 50 to 80 feet away). The walnut tree exudes an allelopathic (biochemical) compound called juglone, which is capable of inhibiting the growth of other plants.[1] Certain crops like tomatoes and eggplants are susceptive to the effects of juglone including: stunted growth, yellow and or brown leaves, discoloration of the plant's vascular system, wilting and even death.[1] Recently, I solved a neighbor's problem with poorly growing blueberry bushes by removing the walnut tree which was only fifteen feet away from the bushes. Despite the fact that the pH of the soil was in the proper range and the blueberries had adequate nutrition and mulch, they were not growing or producing after a few years. Finally, once the walnut tree was removed, the discoloration of the leaves disappeared, and the blueberry bushes began to grow rapidly and produce fruit.

One thing which you will want to have close to your garden is accessible irrigation, such as an already installed tap. The closer a tap is to your garden; you will spend less money on hoses and less time watering the plants. In the long run, buying a durable and higher quality hose will save you money and aggravation versus buying a cheaper and ineffective hose, which often break and have to be replaced. When it is time to water your plants, avoid overhead watering since constantly wet leaves are more susceptible to diseases. Instead in the early morning or late afternoon/evening, water near the base of the plant. Also, avoid wetting and splashing the soil on the plants since this can also spread diseases.

Moreover, one of the most important criteria for site selection is to make sure the garden is in a well-drained location. It is imperative to avoid a spot where rainwater collects and slowly seeps into the soil. An easy way to test the water infiltration capacity of the soil is to dig a few holes that are a few inches across by about a foot deep in the intended area of your garden. After raining, if the water remains in the holes and drains slowly, this is not a suitable place to grow food. If the ground remains excessively wet, this will cause anaerobic (oxygen deficient) conditions which will negatively affect the ability of the roots to grow. Furthermore, excessively wet soils will increase the likelihood of soil borne diseases caused by fungi such as *Pythium* and *Phytophthora*. These common fungi are responsible for a variety of root rots, blights and wilts including *Phytophthora infestans*, which caused the infamous Irish potato famine of the late 1840s.[2] Thus, it is extremely important before planting a garden to monitor the water infiltration capacity of the soil of the intended site. Ways to improve the water infiltration capacity of the soil are cover cropping, mulching and organic fertilizer amendments like compost, gypsum and manure. However, if you can, it makes more sense to start a garden in a location which already has good soil drainage properties.   Just this growing season, which was unusually wet, the one section of my garden was waterlogged for a few days. As a result, twenty tomatoes and a dozen broccoli plants died from a lack of oxygen. Therefore, to avoid future problems, I am going to install some raised beds in this section so the plants will be grown above the original ground level. If you encounter problems while growing food, do not give up, but rather determine the problem and come up with a solution.   If you cannot find a suitable area with good soil drainage properties, planting in raised beds will help you overcome this problem.

Another potentially damaging element to consider when selecting a garden site is the wind.   Make sure you choose a location which is protected from excessive wind as it can damage and break plants, especially those loaded with fruits or vegetables. Constant exposure to intense winds causes smaller leaves in plants. If the leaves are smaller than normal, then the plant will have less leaf area to generate photosynthesis; the process in which plants take sunlight, water and carbon dioxide to generate energy and oxygen. Smaller leaves mean the plant will have decreased energy for production and a reduced yield of fruits or vegetables. Also, too much wind damages the flowers, making them less appealing to pollinating insects which decreases yields.[3] The plant will lose more water (transpiration) if the wind damages the plant's tissues.[4] This can lead to dehydration while simultaneously causing the plant's leaves to curl, which will negatively affect photosynthesis.[4] Additionally, injured plants are more susceptible to damage by pests and diseases since the wounds serve as entry points. Another negative effect of extreme winds is they can carry soil particles which transmit fungal and bacterial diseases once they make contact with the plants.[5]

If you are unable to choose a garden site which is already protected from excessive winds, you can overcome this by erecting a fence, wall or a living permeable barrier such as a hedgerow. When wind hits solid walls, the speed actually tends to increase as the wind travels over the wall and reaches the other side. Therefore, permeable fencing and evergreen hedgerows are a great option since they slow the wind down as the wind passes through the hedgerow or the holes in the fence. If you intend to use a living hedgerow, make sure to plant multiple native species in the hedgerow to reduce the likelihood of pests and or diseases destroying the entire hedgerow. Furthermore, select hedgerow species which deer, groundhogs and rabbits do not eat.

Since my gardens are located along the edges of wide open fields that are exposed to high winds from certain directions, I do a few things to reduce the wind's negative effects on my crops. First, I erect a permeable six foot high metal fence with a permeable privacy screening attached to the side of my garden which receives the most intense wind. Planting taller crops like corn or raspberries on the side which receives the heavier wind is also effective. These methods help slow the wind down before it reaches the other crops. Choosing a garden site which is protected from the wind and or erecting a barrier to control the wind are worth the planning and initial investment. In field studies by the University of Nebraska, numerous vegetables such as bell peppers and snap beans had substantially more yields and a higher market value due to fewer diseases like bacterial leaf spot when grown in wind protected areas versus open fields.[3]

The Importance of Soil pH

One of the most important yet often overlooked planning steps is to take a soil test to determine the pH of the soil and the approximate nutrients in the soil. Knowing the soil pH is critical for many reasons. For instance, most plants prefer a neutral to slightly acidic soil pH, ranging from 6 to 6.8. In *Elements of the Nature and Properties of Soil*, by Nyle C. Brady and Ray R. Weil, they explain how acidic soil conditions can cause an excess uptake of non-nutrient elements like aluminum.[6] When plants acquire too much aluminum, it causes necrosis (death) of the roots and also affects the plant's DNA (deoxyribonucleic acid) and ATP (adenosine triphosphate).[6] Therefore, this disrupts the growth, functioning, and productivity of the plant. In addition to aluminum, plants can take up a surplus of micro-nutrients from acidic soils like manganese, iron, zinc, and copper to the point where it can cause toxicity to the plants and reduce yields.[6] Concerning the macronutrients like nitrogen and calcium, which are essential for fruit and vegetable development, these are less available to most plants in acidic soils.[6] Overall, when plants which prefer more neutral pH levels are grown in acidic soils, they produce less since they are unable to acquire the more important nutrients like nitrogen and instead are exposed to toxic levels of other elements like aluminum.

Besides causing unfavorable soil conditions for nutrient uptake, pests such as leatherjackets and wireworms are more common in acidic soils.[7] Both of these species damage crops by feeding on the roots, tubers, and stems of plants. When pests puncture and injure plant tissue, these wounds increase the opportunity for other pests, harmful bacteria and fungi to infect the plant. On the other hand, beneficial soil organisms that improve the health of the soil like earthworms are less common in acidic soil.[7] Therefore, it is essential to adjust the soil pH in the year(s) prior to planting your garden. This way, you will be less likely to experience difficulties with the health of your plants. The fewer problems you have with diseases, pests and nutrient deficiencies and or toxicities, the more likely you will enjoy growing food and will continue for many seasons!

How to Take a Soil Test

Now that we have established the importance of determining the pH of the soil, how do we conduct a soil test? The first and least accurate way is to obtain a pH meter and stick it into the soil giving an immediate result. Next, a pH testing kit which uses a color chart can be used. However, the most accurate method is sending a soil sample to a soil testing laboratory. To obtain a soil sample, stick a soil probe into the soil at least six inches and extract. Then add the soil into a bucket and repeat ten to fifteen times randomly over the intended site of your garden. Finally, mix all the soil in the bucket together and place it in a sandwich size bag. Then, send it to a soil testing laboratory such as your local county agricultural extension agent. When they send back the report, you will receive an analysis of the nutrients in your soil, the soil type, and the pH of the soil. Usually included will be recommendations on how to adjust the nutrient levels and pH depending on the crops you intend to grow.

What is Lime?

If the soil pH is not in the proper range for the crops which prefer slightly acidic to neutral pH soil levels (6 to 6.8) then lime is added to the soil to neutralize soil acidity. What is lime? Lime is made from natural rock. The two main types of lime used for gardening are calcitic limestone which is composed of calcium and also dolomitic limestone which contains calcium and magnesium. These can usually be purchased at hardware/gardening stores in 40 lb bags either in the pelletized or pulverized form. The pulverized form is powdery and is faster acting in the soil compared to the pelletized form. However, the pulverized form is dusty, messy and more difficult to spread. The pelletized form which takes longer to react in the soil, is more convenient to handle as it does not make a mess and is easier to spread. Since lime usually takes six months to a year to alter the soil pH, we must apply lime well in advance of planting the garden. If you plan ahead and add lime in the previous year, the soil should have the proper pH once planting season arrives in the spring. This will substantially reduce problems and increase yields, making your growing experience more satisfying. If you have to alter the pH significantly, it is best to do it gradually over a period of time rather than trying to correct it in one application.

How Does Lime Work in the Soil?

The application of lime is going to neutralize soil acidity and increase the soil pH through the following chemical processes. When added to the soil, the lime will react with the carbon dioxide and water in the soil subsequently releasing bicarbonate (HCO_3^-) .[6] Bicarbonate is more neutral than the acidifying properties of carbon dioxide and water.[6] Moreover, the soil is going to release some of the carbon dioxide gas into the atmosphere.[6] Then the more basic properties of calcium (Ca^{2+}) and magnesium (Mg^{2+}) will trade places in the soil with the acidic properties of the hydrogen (H+) and the aluminum (Al^{3+}).[6] In more simple terms, the neutral pH properties of the lime are going to kick out the acidic pH properties in the soil.

What Causes Soil Acidity

One of the most common causes of soil acidity is how rain acidifies the soil. For instance, when carbon dioxide (CO^2) dissolves in the rain it creates carbonic acid, which releases hydrogen ions (H+)

in the soil.[6] Remember from chemistry class that hydrogen is one of the more acidic elements. Many farmers and gardeners have noticed that low lying areas in their fields or gardens which collect more water, tend to be more acidic than the higher areas. Furthermore, the roots of plants and trees release carbon dioxide into the soil.[6] Also, there are more micro-organisms underneath the soil than there are animals above the soil. Since all of these micro-organisms are alive, they exhale carbon dioxide into the soil as a result of their metabolic processes.[6] Once again, the soil is made more acidic when the water and carbon dioxide combine and release carbonic acid and hydrogen ions.

In addition, soil acidity is caused by the decomposition of organic matter such as leaves, grass, mulches, manure and compost.[6] How does this happen? Organic matter forms water soluble relationships with calcium and magnesium.[6] These are the two main ingredients in lime which help to neutralize soil acidity.[6] As a result, these nutrients are more easily washed away as water moves through the soil.[6] Furthermore, the application of organic or synthetic fertilizers releases hydrogen when the nitrogen in the ammonium form (NH_4+) is converted to the plant available form called nitrate (NO_3-).[6] Often the nitrogen in either organic or synthetic fertilizer is in the form of ammonium (NH_4+) which is less available to the plant.[6] Then the micro-organisms in the soil help to break down and convert the nitrogen into the inorganic form nitrate (NO_3-), which is now in state the plants have an easier ability acquiring as a nutrient.[6] During this transformation from ammonium to nitrate, hydrogen is released into the soil causing soil acidity.[6] Also, the decomposition of sulfur by micro-organisms releases sulfuric acid (H_2SO_4).[6] Where does this sulfur come from? Sulfur is one of the components of the proteins found in various plant parts such as the leaves and branches.[6] Then as these sulfur containing parts fall and are decomposed in the soil, this releases sulfuric acid.[6]

Plants can also acidify the soil based on the manner in which they acquire nutrients. For example, plants take up nutrients from the soil which are either in the negative state such as NO_3- (nitrate) or in the positive state such as K+ (potassium).[6] In order to maintain a flow of nutrients, plants want there to be equilibrium of positive and negative charges in the soil.[6] Therefore, if they take up more negative charged nutrients, the plants themselves release hydrogen into the soil to maintain this charge equilibrium.[6] Recall that hydrogen is one of the main causes of soil acidity. Combined together, these are the most common factors which increase the acidity of the soil. Thus, since the processes which cause soil acidity are continuous, liming the soil will have to occur yearly or every few years based on the recommendations in the soil test report.

Cover Crops

Another soil enhancing step you can do before you plant a garden is to plant fall or spring cover crop species such as alfalfa, clover, oats, peas, forage radish, rye and hairy vetch. Cover crops are unique crops which are grown for their soil enriching properties. Why are cover crops so valuable? Certain cover crops have the ability to add important nutrients, like nitrogen, to the soil. For instance, legumes like alfalfa, clover, hairy vetch, and peas have a special symbiotic relationship with nitrogen fixing bacteria called Rhizobia. Amazingly, the Rhizobia have the incredible ability to transform nitrogen in the atmosphere (which plants cannot use) to the plant available form of nitrogen in the soil.

Then, when the cover crops die, the remainder of nutrients found in the leaves and stems will slowly decompose and gradually release organic fertilizer throughout the growing season and beyond. This process will usually insure that the crops you plant will have a steady supply of nutrients. Moreover, this will reduce fertilizer costs during the growing season while lowering pollution. The production of inorganic fertilizers uses a great deal of fossil fuels. The less fertilizer you have to buy, the less fuel, resources, and packaging are used to make the fertilizer and ship it around the world to your backyard.

In addition to adding fertilizer to the soil, cover crops reduce pollution by their ability to sequester or capture nutrients which can prevent them from being washed away in the soil. For instance, according to Brady and Weil:

"…the greatest potential for leaching of nitrate from cropland occurs during the fall, winter, and early spring, after harvest and
before planting of the main crop. During this time of vulnera-
bility, an actively growing cover crop will reduce percolation
of water and remove much of the nitrogen from the water that

does not percolate, incorporating this nutrient into plant tissue".[6]

Once again, when the cover crops which sequestered nutrients like nitrogen from the soil are killed, the nitrogen and other nutrients in the plant tissue will slowly breakdown and be released as fertilizer throughout the growing season. They also explain how cover crops like oats and forage radish sequester more nutrients compared to legumes like clover since the oats and forage radish have faster root development during the fall.[6] The best choice for optimum soil health is a combination of multiple types of cover crops like legumes and grasses which provide both nitrogen fixation and sequestering of nutrients.

Reducing Eutrophication (Pollution of Watershed)

Cover crops are also beneficial because they have lower levels of phosphorous compared to other fertilizers, including organic fertilizer like compost and manure.[6] If phosphorus is an essential macro-nutrient for plants, why is it bad to have too much phosphorus in the soil? When there is an excess of phosphorus in the soil, it has the potential to leach into groundwater, streams, rivers, lakes, ponds, bays and the ocean (the watershed) causing serious environmental pollution called eutrophication.[6] As this phosphorous accumulates in the water, it leads to an increase in the growth of algae.[8] According to James E. Cloern from a report in the Marine Ecology Research Series: "...since algal growth rates are often naturally limited by the availability of N or P, then   fertilization of estuarine-coastal waters with these elements will stimulate the growth, biomass accumulation and primary production of the phytoplankton community".[8] Therefore, it is the escalating land application in recent decades of both synthetic and organic fertilizers containing high levels of phosphorous and nitrogen which is causing an increase in eutrophication when it leaches into the watershed.

What is the big deal about some extra growth of algae in the water; are we not focusing on growing plants and food? A report by NOAA, The U.S. National Oceanographic and Atmospheric Administration, explains how this increase in algal blooms causes a shortage of oxygen in the water which negatively affects aquatic species of plants and vertebrates like fish.[9] For instance, as the increased algal blooms die, they sink to the bottom. Then the micro-organisms, which decay plant matter, consume the oxygen in the water and use it as fuel to help decompose the dead algae. As the amount of decaying plant material increases, the numbers of micro-organisms increase. Simultaneously, this decreases the amount of oxygen in the water, making it unavailable for fish and other marine vertebrates. Resulting from the lack of oxygen, fish and other marine vertebrates end up dying in large numbers.

This report also demonstrates how long term algal blooms block sunlight which can kill submerged aquatic plant species.[9] These aquatic plant species provide both food and habitat for fish and other marine vertebrates.[9] Thus, fish and marine vertebrates are negatively affected by a lack of oxygen, habitat and food as a result of eutrophication. Additionally, the report explains how eutrophication is directly affecting humans:

> "These eutrophic symptoms are indicative of degraded water quality conditions that can adversely affect the use of estuarine resources, including commercial and recreational fishing, boating, swimming, and tourism. Eutrophic symptoms may also cause risks to human health, including serious illness and death, that result from the consumption of shellfish
> contaminated with algal toxins, or from direct exposure to waterborne or airborne toxins".[9]

Therefore, the increasing rates of nutrient runoff, like phosphorous, into watersheds around the world is affecting not only marine species, but also humans, both economically and biologically. Thus, reducing nutrient runoff from your farm or garden through methods like planting cover crops, can decrease your negative effect on the environment. Combined with sustainable food growing practices by other gardeners and farmers, we all have the ability to improve the health of ourselves and the planet. When you grow your own food, you can manage how you use fertilizers and what methods you use to reduce pollution. Thus, you have greater control over how your diet will affect the earth, versus an individual who buys their food off somebody else whose growing practices they have little or no control over.

How Cover Crops Improve the Soil

In addition to adding and sequestering nutrients in the soil, cover crops improve the physical quality of the soil in a number of ways. For example, one of the worst things is to leave the soil bare and exposed. Consider trying to live without your skin; it would be impossible! Thus, we should regard bare soil to be just as deadly as if we did not have skin. As water and rain drops contact bare soil, it causes erosion and displacement of soil particles and nutrients. Though the rain drops are small, since they are falling far from the sky, their velocity is so powerful that when they hit the soil, they displace it and cause it to wash away. Soil formation itself is a process which takes a very long time. However, when the soil is bare, nature's work can be washed away in one rainstorm. How many times during rainstorms have you seen brown water flowing along the side of a field, road, or from a yard? Unfortunately, that is an example of valuable soil being eroded by the force of the water. The washing away of the soil removes precious organic matter and nutrients. Eventually this contributes to eutrophication of the watershed when these nutrients and sediments settle in a lake, pond etc. Fortunately, the planting of cover crops can help cover the soil after the fall harvest. Additionally, certain cover crops start to grow earlier in the spring, thus providing earlier soil coverage. With greater soil coverage, there will be more plant particles to help reduce the effects of raindrops displacing soil and causing erosion. Simultaneously, this will slow down water moving horizontally over the soil surface which will reduce erosion.

According to Sustainable Agriculture Research and Education (SARE), cover crops, "Increase the soil's ability to absorb and hold water, through improvement in pore structure, thereby preventing large quantities of water from moving across the soil surface".[10] These cover crops will slow down the speed of horizontally-moving water, and also help to increase the water infiltration capacity of the soil. Increased pore space in the soil helps nutrients, air, and plant roots to move more easily throughout the soil. In addition to improving the water infiltration capacity of the soil, certain cover crops like tillage radish have the ability to reduce soil compaction by breaking through compacted layers of soil with deep infiltrating roots. If you are planting a garden in the corner of your yard, chances are the soil is compacted from foot traffic and equipment like lawn mowers. Also, if you are planting a garden in a field like I do, years of large farm tractors riding on the land have most likely compacted the soil. Furthermore, after years of plowing and planting in a field or using a tiller in a garden, a "plow pan" forms. This occurs at the bottommost layer where the plow/tiller reaches and forms a hard compacted layer of soil. Just like when you use a shovel to dig a hole, the edge of the hole becomes compacted, the same thing happens underground as plows and tillers move horizontally across the soil. Plow pans not only reduce water infiltration, but they greatly impede the ability of plant's roots to infiltrate through this hard layer of soil. Therefore, planting cover crops with deep roots like tillage radish is important to break up soil compaction and to increase the water infiltration capacity of the soil.

How Cover Crops Increase Organic Matter in the Soil

Just as you need to eat on a daily basis, consider organic matter as being food for the soil. Why is organic matter so important for the soil? According to SARE, "The benefits of organic matter include improved soil structure, increased infiltration and water-holding capacity, increased cation exchange capacity (the ability of the soil to act as a short-term storage bank for positively charged plant nutrients) and more efficient long-term storage of nutrients".[10] How does organic matter improve soil structure? Organic matter provides food and habitat for soil organisms like earthworms, bacteria, and fungi. The increase in soil organisms is going to increase the aggregation of the soil which is one of the most critical components of healthy soil. What is soil aggregation? As demonstrated by the USDA Natural Resources Conservation Service, soil aggregation is when particles of soil form a strong attachment to one another.[11] This allows for more pore space in the soil, which makes it easier for plant roots to grow and increases water infiltration and retention while also reducing erosion.[11] The USDA article also explains how if strong aggregates are not formed in the soil, the soil is more likely to be displaced by rain and water.[11] When rain falls on soil with poor cover/aggregation, these individual soil particles can then form a crust on the soil surface.[11] This soil crust adversely affects the ability of plants to grow and reduces the ability of water and air to enter the soil.[11] Once again, this will lead to more soil erosion which is going to cause a removal of organic matter and nutrients and an increase in eutrophication. How do soil organisms help increase soil aggregation? According to Brady and Weil, "Among the biological processes of aggregation, the most prominent are (1) the burrowing and molding activities of soil animals, (2) the enmeshment of particles by sticky networks of roots and fungal hyphae, and (3) the production of organic glues by microorganisms, especially bacteria and fungi".[6]

Thus, organic matter will provide soil animals like earthworms with food. When they release this as casts (poop), the cast will contain plant available sources of nutrients. Also, the sticky casts will help to keep the soil together (aggregation). If there is more food for earthworms, then there will be more burrows and channels in the soil. Therefore, this will result in more water infiltration capacity for the soil. The addition of organic matter to the soil also supports an increase in fungi and bacteria. They too increase soil aggregation by releasing adhesive substances in the soil. For instance, one of the by-products of the micro-organisms' digestion of organic matter are polysaccharides or sticky sugars which help to keep soil particles intact.[6] Furthermore, fungi increase soil aggregation by forming a sticky root like structure that spreads throughout the soil.[6] This underground network helps decompose organic matter and also enhances the uptake of water and nutrients for plants by forming a symbiotic relationship with the plants. By providing sugars and energy to the fungi, the plant helps the fungi to survive. Then, the fungi roots, which are smaller than the plant's roots, can access hard to reach places. This increases the plant's uptake of nutrients and water up to ten times versus if the plant did not have this symbiotic relationship with the fungi.

Obviously planting cover crops is one of the most beneficial things you can do to improve the health of the soil and the overall environment. Whether or not you are just beginning to grow food or if you have been doing so for many years, it is an excellent idea to utilize cover crops. This upcoming spring, I will plant cover crops in a whole new section of a field where I intend to put an additional garden. By next growing season, my new garden site will be healthier since I am planting cover crops rather than if I just decided to plant a garden without taking the aforementioned steps. Then after the fall harvest, I will plant cover crops where my garden has been for the last two years in order to give the soil a break and also to improve the soil. I will allow these cover crops to grow in this old garden for a year or two before resuming planting in this area. This will this improve the health of the soil and reduce the chances for an outbreak of diseases and pests since this is a form of crop rotation. When it comes to the fall planting of cover crops, make sure there is enough time for the cover crop to get established before winter kill. If there is not enough time, then use some kind of mulch like straw or woodchips to cover the bare soil which will help prevent soil erosion while adding organic matter to the soil.

In this short yet thorough chapter, you have learned the importance of site selection, testing and adjusting pH levels, planting cover crops, reducing eutrophication and the value of organic matter. These processes are often overlooked yet are so essential for establishing a healthy garden. If the soil is healthy before you even plant, then your plants will also be healthy. If your plants are healthy then you will be healthier, since you will be more likely to continue growing food if you have a positive experience the first year.

Chapter 2: Fencing, Fertilizing, and Tilling

Fencing

A common excuse people say that caused them to quit growing food is because animals like deer, rabbits, and groundhogs ate their crops. Often, these same people will admit that they did not even bother to set up a fence, or they only built one a few feet high. If you do not take the time and effort to set up a proper fence, one animal can literally eat and destroy your entire garden in a short amount of time. To prevent this and to enjoy the fruits of your labor, to reap what you sow, you must set up a well constructed fence before you even plant.

Concerning fencing, what I have discovered is the age old adage, "you get what you pay for". You should make a long-term investment by building a garden fence that is the "Fort Knox" of garden fences. For the first few years, I took the easier and "cheaper" way out. For instance, I used small to medium sized trees I cut down in the woods as fence posts. Even if you tar the bottom and use durable trees like Locust or Oak, they usually rot faster than metal posts. By the time you cut the trees down, transport and amend them, then use a post-hole- digger to dig in the ground, you have devoted a considerable amount of time and work. Instead, for about $7 each, I purchase seven-foot-high metal fence posts. I prefer to use metal fence posts than wooden ones since metal is more stable in the ground and lasts longer. When you stake them into the ground, make sure to go a foot deep so the post is extra secure. To stake the posts, I stand on a step ladder or chair and use a sledge hammer. Please make sure to wear eye protection since sometimes bits of metal can break off and potentially injure your eyes. For stability and economic purposes, I find it is best to place the posts every four to six feet.

Concerning the actual fencing, again if you pay more you get more. In the beginning, I bought seven-foot-high plastic deer fencing. While 100 feet of plastic fence costs $50 compared to 50 feet of heavy duty metal fencing for $65, you will spend more money in the long run if you buy the cheaper plastic fencing since it will have to be replaced. For instance, the biggest problem with the plastic fencing is its susceptibility to destruction by lawn equipment. It easily gets broken by the weed whacker. Also, it gets chopped up by the lawn mower, potentially getting tangled in the mower and causing serious damage to your lawn equipment. I have even heard of lawn mowers catching fire because of the plastic fencing getting overheated while stuck in the mower. Furthermore, plastic fencing is susceptible to the effects of winter. For example, the weight of the snow and ice causes damage. Another serious problem I have witnessed are groundhogs chewing through the fencing. All it takes is one or two groundhogs to get into your garden to destroy everything for which you worked so hard. Usually within two or three years, I have had to replace the plastic fencing taking up more time and money.

After learning from experience, I now buy six-foot-high thick metal fencing. While the cheapest I could buy was $65 for 50 feet, the advantages are that it will last longer than plastic fencing. Also, the metal fencing is so strong the groundhogs cannot chew threw it. Moreover, it does not break from the elements and or while you are weed whacking or mowing the grass. Another important yet overlooked step is to secure the bottom of the fencing to prevent animals from burrowing underneath. To do so, I use thick, four-feet-high poultry fencing. I take the lower foot and curve it outwards along the bottom of the main fencing and the ground, so that it extends a foot from the perimeter of the original garden fence. Now there is double fencing at the bottom few feet of your garden which should effectively keep unwanted animals out. If an animal tries to burrow into the ground, they will be unable to penetrate this metal fencing. Then, based on your preference, bury this bottom layer with soil, stones, mulch or woodchips. I avoid stones since they can potentially ruin your lawn equipment if you accidentally mow over them. Thus, my preferred choice is woodchips since they also prevent weeds from growing. It is easier to make sure animals are not burrowing under your fencing if you do not allow any vegetation to grow along the fence edge. However, in certain areas like the entrance to my garden, I enjoy planting perennial wildflowers and sunflowers along the fence edge since they create a breathtaking view and help attract pollinators like bees.

Now that you have properly built the "Fort Knox" of garden fences the right way the first year, you will save time and money in the long run. Unlike my younger self, you will avoid multiple fence projects each season, year after year. One of the things I disliked most about growing food during my first years was how much labor, time and money I spent on fencing with inefficient results. I have also learned from trial and error, how important it is to establish a fence for your garden or orchard well in advance of planting time. Take advantage of late fall or early spring months to get the fencing done and out of the way. This is a wonderful time to complete this project since there is not much one can plant or grow during this time of year. Unfortunately, I used to fence and plant within the same time leading to a great deal of labor and moments of doubt, discouragement, and frustration. By avoiding my mistakes, your experience with growing food will be more enjoyable and you will be more likely to continue doing it for a long period of time.

Buying a Garden Tiller

In my sixth year of growing food, I purchased my first heavy duty 17 inch wide Husqvarna Garden Tiller for $800. I wish I bought one earlier since it has made my gardening experience more efficient and enjoyable. Once again, since this is a lifetime investment, if you pay more for a quality product, you will get more in the long run. I know plenty of individuals who purchased a heavy duty garden tiller that still works decades later. Often, the cheapest tillers only last a few years. They also do not have the power or performance of the more expensive and better built brands. If you do not want to buy one, garden tillers can be rented from local garden and power equipment stores. Usually the ones they rent to people are the more heavy duty brands since they know people will misuse and abuse it. Thus, the rented models are highly efficient since stores trust them enough to rent them to everyday customers. That is why I bought a brand new version of the same model the store rents to its customers since I knew it was well trusted and tested.

Before I bought my own garden tiller, my good neighbor Farmer Jim would plow and disc my garden plot with his tractor. Unfortunately, at once I had a very large area to fence, plant, mulch and weed. Since the tractor is so large and requires plenty of room to operate, I had to take the fencing down at the end of each year. Then, I had to re-fence everything after the soil was plowed, disked and cultivated which took so much time and effort during planting time.

Now since I bought my own tiller, I can leave my fencing up which saves me a great deal of time and effort and makes the planting experience more enjoyable. Moreover, plowing and turning over the entire garden at once is nonsensical because of the varying planting schedules of different plants. Ideally, beginning in early spring four to six weeks before the last expected frost, you can plant cool weather crops like peas and onions. Then in May crops like potatoes and broccoli can be planted. Finally, after the last expected spring frost, you can plant crops like cucumbers, peppers, and tomatoes.

By turning the whole soil over at once in a 100 foot by 100 foot garden, I was inundated with a sense of urgency and an overwhelming necessity of labor. Not only did I have to fence and plant the whole area at once, but I had to worry about weeding and using a great deal of mulch like straw, hay, and wood chips to prevent weeds from growing. Obtaining mulches in bulk and spreading them at once can be expensive and time consuming. The average person will not enjoy their gardening experience if they do it the manner I did during my first few years. Luckily, the following planting method will help save time, effort and money and will conserve the soil.

Zone Tilling

Since I obtained my own garden tiller, instead of turning over and cultivating all of the soil in the garden at once, I can now practice a form of conservation tillage called zone tilling. Zone tilling is the process where you only till the soil in the rows where you are planting your crops. Therefore, the soil in between the rows is not tilled and is left intact. Zone tilling significantly reduces the destruction of the soil. For instance, every time the soil is turned over and disturbed, the soil's exposure to oxygen increases soil micro-organism activity which facilitates a more rapid decomposition of the organic matter in the soil.[1] According to the United States Department of Agriculture, "Excessive tillage destroys soil aggregates increasing the rate of soil organic matter decomposition. Stable soil aggregates increase active organic matter and protect stable organic matter from rapid microbial decomposition".[2] Therefore, an excess of soil disturbance through plowing and tilling in the same area year after year, can rapidly remove the organic matter and nutrients in the soil. Moreover, if organic matter like compost, mulches, and manures are not being added to the soil each year, then the organic matter in the soil will be rapidly depleted. Zone tilling also reduces the likelihood of soil erosion from the forces of the wind and water.

How does this happen? Since zone tilling leaves the soil in between the rows intact, there is less soil bare and exposed and more organic matter left on the soil surface. A top layer of organic matter on the soil significantly reduces soil erosion by slowing down the rate water passes over the soil, the ability of raindrops to disperse soil particles on bare soil, and the wind's effect on soil erosion.[1] Though raindrops are tiny, because of the distance they fall from the sky, the speed at which they hit the soil is strong enough to displace the soil and cause erosion. Zone tilling also reduces the rate water passes over the soil surface because it disturbs less of the vast networks of burrows and channels that soil organisms like earthworms have created in the soil. These burrows are important since they increase the water infiltration capacity of the soil. Additionally, the earthworms help to transport organic matter from the soil surface to deeper underground, where it eventually becomes nutrients for the soil and plants.

Before you till the garden, make sure to mow down the cover crop, grass, and or weeds. In one of my early years of growing food, I neglected to keep the vegetation mowed in my garden plot before planting. Then Farmer Jim purposely plowed and disked the soil to teach me how much more difficult it is to work with the soil if you do not mow the vegetation beforehand. It makes it much harder to break up the soil since the plants are bulkier and they tend to get caught in the equipment. Then when you try to dig holes to plant, it seems there is more bulky plant material in the way rather than having workable soil.

In addition to mowing the vegetation, you can use an herbicide about a week before you plant your vegetables. While herbicides tend to get a bad reputation, I believe if you use them in moderation (like most things in life), they can be beneficial. For instance, if you do not use an herbicide and just mow the vegetation, all it takes is for a little of the roots of the vegetation to still be intact and they will soon start to re-grow after you plant your vegetables. However, if you use an herbicide which kills down to the root, these weeds will not re-grow and your vegetables will have a better head start than the weeds.

Then by the time weeds start to re-grow (if they do), the vegetables will be so tall they should help to block the sunlight and prevent the weeds from growing. Another benefit of the herbicides is how it turns the vegetation in-between the rows into a source of fertilizer and mulch. This will help to reduce soil erosion and prevent weeds from growing. Furthermore, as the vegetation dies and decomposes, it will slowly release nutrients back into the soil making them available for the plants. To further enhance the soil and stall the re-growth of weeds in-between the rows, I add a few inch layer of mulch like woodchips, straw or grass clippings.

If you do not want to use herbicides, you can use plastic tarps for about a week to kill the vegetation or just mow the vegetation down. After you have tilled your rows, try to remove as many of the plant roots in these rows before you plant your vegetables. While they may look dead because they are broken up, you will be amazed at how rapidly these broken up plant roots will start to re-grow. Just like if you use herbicides, mulch immediately after planting your vegetables since this help deters the growth of weeds. If the area in between the rows is not sprayed with an herbicide, it will still be alive and will need to be cut throughout the growing season. Then, as needed, use a push mower to mow in between the rows of plants. The constant cutting and addition of the mowed plant debris into the rows of the vegetables adds organic matter and fertilizer throughout the growing season. However, be careful to not let the vegetation in between the rows go to seed and then mow it since you will only be mowing weed seeds into the vegetable rows. One of the principles of effective weed management is to prevent weeds from going to seed in order to reduce the number of viable weed seeds in the soil.

For the past few years I have practiced zone tilling and I am still amazed how much time and effort it saves compared to my previous methods of gardening! I was used to spending so much time weeding and mulching that I almost felt like something was wrong. I had all this extra time on my hands since I did not have to weed so much. Overall, I found the herbicide method plus zone tilling and mulching to be more effective than just mowing the vegetation, zone tilling and mulching.

Fertilizers

Another important topic to consider before it is time to plant your garden is what kind of fertilizers you want to use. As you have already learned, cover crops are one of the best fertilizers. They naturally add and sequester nutrients, reduce soil erosion, add organic matter to the soil and have more sustainable levels of phosphorus in comparison to organic fertilizers like compost and manure. I prefer using a combination of cover cropping, organic and inorganic fertilizers. Inorganic fertilizers (such as 10-10-10) increase the rate of nutrient cycling which makes nutrients more available to plants.[1] A common misconception is that inorganic fertilizers directly feed the plants. Rather, they help plants by freeing up the nutrients in the soil which are often in the passive state or being utilized by micro-organisms as energy to help digest organic matter.[1] Thus, if a plant is experiencing a serious nutrient deficiency during the growing season, using an inorganic fertilizer will almost instantaneously supply nutrients. However, an organic fertilizer would take a longer time to break down and become available to the plant. Unlike organic fertilizers such as compost and manure, inorganic fertilizers do not add valuable organic matter to the soil.

If you are going to use inorganic fertilizers, when and how should they be applied? Generally, you should use them during the period of the most rapid nutrient uptake by the plant. For most summer annuals, like peppers and tomatoes, applying a small amount at planting and then the main amount four to six weeks after planting is ideal.[1] For trees, the best application timing is a few weeks before and when new leaves are forming.[1] There are different ways to incorporate the inorganic fertilizer into the soil. The first and most obvious way is to broadcast it over the soil surface of the entire growing area. However, this increases the possibility that water will cause leaching of the fertilizer into the watershed which can cause eutrophication. Unfortunately, this method also provides fertilizer for weeds which will make them grow faster.

Localized placement of fertilizer is the preferred method if you want to reduce the negative effects fertilizers can have on the environment and to feed less weeds. At planting time, a starter fertilizer can be applied in the soil at least 5 cm below and or 5 cm to the side of the plant.[1] Be careful not to have the fertilizer too close to or in contact with the roots since it can burn the roots and potentially kill the plant. Then during the period of rapid nutrient uptake (which will vary for each crop), place more fertilizer into the soil around the plant and cover it up. This period usually begins when the fruit or vegetable begins to appear on the plant. Interestingly, a plant can acquire a substantial amount of its nutrients even if only a small amount of the plant's roots are in contact with the fertilizer! By using the localized placement method, this will reduce pollution by preventing the leaching of the fertilizer into the watershed. Moreover, localized placement means less weeds will be fertilized. In comparison to broadcasting fertilizer on the surface which tends to make the fertilizer available only in the upper part of the soil, localized placement will increase the amount of nutrients available in the plant's root zone. Furthermore, localized placement of fertilizer should reduce the amount of overall fertilizer purchased and used since it is not being broadcasted over the entire area. Overall, this method saves time, money, and the environment.

How to Make Compost

If you plan to use organic fertilizers such as compost and manure, then once again it pays to plan ahead. It is important to apply them in advance of planting so the nutrients in the manure or compost can be transformed by soil microbes into the plant available form. Since compost can take from weeks to months to make, this is another process which can be done before you even plant your garden. To make compost, gather materials high in nitrogen like: animal manure (avoid cat and dog), grass clippings, weeds (before going to seed) and kitchen wastes like banana peels and coffee grinds. It is recommended to have ¼ of the pile to contain these "greens" with a low carbon to nitrogen ratio. The next ¾ of the compost pile should contain "brown" material with a high carbon to nitrogen ratio such as: newspapers, cardboard, leaves, pine needles, straw, hay, and wood shavings from non-chemically treated wood.

Then before combining this material into a pile, make sure to cut bulkier items into smaller pieces. Furthermore, shred material like paper since this will increase the surface area and thus the rate of decomposition. Afterwards, incorporate the material into piles at least three feet wide by three feet tall in a well aerated and not too sunny location. Avoid hot and sunny locations since this can dry the compost pile and volatilize the nutrients in the compost. It is also important to water the material as it is being mixed and to keep the compost pile wet. A good rule of thumb is you do not want the compost too wet so that when squeezed, it lets water out like a sponge. Making sure there is adequate air flow in and around the pile is important since aeration will expose the material to oxygen which is going to help increase the rate of decomposition. It is essential to turn the compost pile at least once a week. If the pile is too wet, it helps to turn it on a hot sunny day. On the contrary, if the pile needs to be watered, it is a wonderful idea to turn the compost while it is raining. Not only will this save labor but you also get to enjoy the smell of the rain while singing in the rain!

In order to decompose rapidly and efficiently, the compost pile should be at least three feet tall by three feet wide. Moreover, as long as adequate moisture and aeration are maintained and if the pile is turned and mixed about once a week, then the pile will gradually decompose into usable compost. The decomposition process involves several stages. For instance, in the beginning mesophilic stage, simple sugars and easily dissolved particles break down and increase the heat of the pile to around 40 degrees Celsius or 104 degrees Fahrenheit.[1] The next stage is called the thermophilic stage, when denser materials like cellulose are decomposed, generating temperatures between 50 degrees Celsius to 75 degrees Celsius or 122 degrees Fahrenheit to 167 degrees Fahrenheit.[1] The final stage is known as the curing stage when temperatures return to normal. Amazingly, beneficial micro-organisms which kill plant pathogens and help plants grow begin to appear in the pile during this stage.[1] For instance, a unique fungus found in compost called *Arthobotyrs anchonia* traps plant harming nematodes and kills them.[1] These nematodes spread plant diseases by using their parasitic jaws to bite and infect the roots of plants. Thus, reducing these nematodes by using compost will certainly improve the health of your plants.

Benefits of Compost

What are the other benefits of using compost? According to the Environmental Protection Agency, Americans in 2012 threw out 251 million tons of trash, of which 87 million tons or 34.5% was recycled.[3] This buildup of organic matter in the landfills eventually creates methane gas (CH_4). When released into the atmosphere, methane gas is estimated to be 25 times more powerful as a greenhouse gas than carbon dioxide.[1] Methane traps more heat from the sun's rays than carbon dioxide so composting this material instead of throwing it away in landfills can have a positive environmental impact.

Another way compost helps to reduce greenhouse emissions is through its carbon neutral composition; in other words, the materials used in the compost have been recently alive compared to other soil amendments like peat.[1] Peat is made from organic material that has been decomposing underground for up to thousands of years. Therefore, when it is mined, the carbon in the organic matter which has been sustainably sequestered by nature will be re-exposed to the air and release carbon dioxide, methane and other greenhouse gases.[4] The mining process itself, plus the shipment of the peat across the globe to your backyard, uses a considerable amount of fossil fuels and packaging material. Compost further reduces pollution since it tends to release less nitrous oxide (N_2O), a powerful greenhouse gas, than inorganic fertilizers like ammonia.[4]

In smaller amounts, compost can help to mitigate pollution by reducing leaching of nutrients. For example, the surface of humified organic matter has the ability to hold more nutrients and water than other types of soil particles.[4] Compost is an effective way to convert materials like grass and leaves into a beneficial soil amendment. However, since compost tends to have higher ratios of nitrogen and phosphorous, overusing it can have detrimental environmental effects, including eutrophication of the watershed.[1] Relying on compost as a sole means of fertilizer and soil enhancement can have potentially negative environmental effects. Furthermore, the nutrients in compost are not readily available to plants when it is applied to the soil. Thus, it makes sense to use compost in smaller doses over a gradual period of time. Overall composting can reduce pollution and will save you money by lowering your garbage disposal bill and by lowering the amount of soil amendments like peat and fertilizer that you will have to buy.

Manure

Besides adding valuable organic matter to the soil and enhancing soil micro-organism and earthworm activity, animal manure is beneficial since about 75% of the nitrogen, 80% of the phosphorus and 90% of the potassium in the animal's diet ends up in the manure.[1] Since animal manure is rich in nutrients, it is essential, just like with other fertilizers, to incorporate it into the soil. This will prevent volatilization of the nutrients into the atmosphere and leaching of the nutrients into the watershed. Interestingly, to get the same amount of nitrogen from manure versus chemical fertilizer, you would have to use 20x the amount of manure![5] Therefore, this is why I am a proponent of using both inorganic and organic fertilizers to reduce pollution and to increase both the nutrients and organic matter in the soil. When using animal manures (avoid cat and dog), make sure to apply it weeks and months before harvest to reduce the likelihood of contracting manure related diseases. Be careful when using horse manure since it can spread weed seeds. Also, you have to allow all manure to "cure" or to sit and decompose for some time. This will help make sure it is not too "hot", or rich in nutrients which can be detrimental to plants. Overall, an advantage of using manure is that it will greatly enhance soil organic matter and soil micro-organism activity.

From selecting a proper site, testing and adjusting the soil pH, utilizing cover crops, reducing pollution, setting up proper fencing, making and using compost, practicing zone tilling, the importance and function of organic matter, and the differences between organic and inorganic fertilizers, you are now well informed on a wide variety of topics. Understanding this information is essential for respecting and improving the soil and the earth. Now that you recognize the importance and the biology of healthy soil, you are obligated to be a steward of the soil and the earth. As you are working in the garden, you will understand how practicing sustainable growing methods enhances your health and the health of the environment.

Chapter 3: Crop Rotation, Mulching, and Succession Planting

Regardless of where you live or what you intend to grow, one of the most important aspects of growing food is to practice crop rotation. Crop rotation is the intentional planting of different, non-related crops in the same area for successive years. Why is crop rotation so important? Planting the same crop year after year in the same place will negatively affect the soil and decrease production through a number of ways.

For example, crops have different nutrient requirements, some preferring certain nutrients more than others. If a crop like corn which requires a great deal of nitrogen is repeatedly planted in one area, it will rapidly deplete the soil of this nutrient. Luckily, rotating crops lessens the chances that the soil will experience nutrient deficiencies. Additionally, consider the disturbance of the soil which results from having to plow, till, disc, and cultivate the soil year after year. As aforementioned, this turning and mixing of the soil profile is going to increase oxidation and microbial activity. Resulting, this will accelerate the decomposition of organic matter in the soil.

Certain crops like potatoes create more soil disturbance than other crops because of their unique growing requirements. To start, the ground is cultivated to plant the potatoes. Then as the potatoes grow, you have to cultivate the soil alongside of them and mound it up in hills around the potato plant. Often the "hilling" of potatoes occurs a few times a season. Finally, the harvest of potatoes disturbs the soil profile since they have to be dug up from the ground. Unless the soil is immediately covered with mulch or a cover crop, this bare soil is vulnerable to erosion by the rain and snow. If you plant crops like potatoes that dramatically disturb the soil profile in the same place for continuous years, it will have negative effects on the soil. Thus, it makes sense to rotate the different annual crops you grow in the same location.

To further enhance the benefits of crop rotation, you should allow the area where you grow your food to experience a "fallow" by planting long-term perennials like cover crops. These crops will give the soil a break from the constant plowing, tilling and disturbance of the soil profile associated with annuals like potatoes. While perennials are growing, there is less chance for soil erosion since their deep fibrous roots tend to hold the soil together. Recall that some of these cover crops even add and sequester nutrients to the soil. To maximize results, a crop rotation plan which cycles a variety of annual and perennial crops will improve the health of the soil.

How Crop Rotation Reduces Diseases and Pests

Crop rotation is one of the most effective ways to naturally reduce the likelihood of diseases and pests. If one crop (or its relative) is planted year after year in the same place, this increases the chances for an infestation of pests and or an outbreak of diseases. Though there are different types of plants, they can be related members of the same taxonomic family. This is crucial to understand, since diseases and pests which are attracted to a certain plant will also be attracted to other plants within the same family. For example, eggplant, peppers, potatoes and tomatoes are all classified into the *Solanaceae* family. Another common plant family is the *Brassicaceae*, including broccoli, cabbage, cauliflower, kohlrabi, mustard, radishes, rutabagas, and turnips. The *Curcubitaceae* family includes cucumbers, gourds, melons, and summer and winter squash.

Regarding the pests affecting the *Solanaceae* family, one of the most destructive is the Colorado Potato Beetle. Though its primary food source is potatoes, it can also feast upon other members of the *Solanaceae* family like peppers, tomatoes and eggplant. Therefore, avoid planting members of one plant family next to or in the same area where members of that family are currently or were recently being grown. When can you re-plant a crop or its family members in a similar location? It is advised to wait three to four years. If crop rotation is not practiced, then pests like the Colorado Potato Beetle will be more likely to reach infestation levels.

How does this happen? If potatoes are planted for the first time, chances are there will not be a major problem with the Colorado Potato Beetle. While there may only be a few of these pests, they will most likely breed and lay eggs. Then, upon being born in the following year, these pests will not have to travel far for food and mates if crop rotation is not being practiced. This cycle will continue and get worse over the seasons. Even if after a few years crop rotation is finally implemented, the amount of pests will be so high they will most likely find the new areas where the potatoes are being planted. Then you will have to deal with increased financial costs from damage to the crops and also for the time and labor spent on trying to control the pests.

All of this mayhem regardless of where you live or the types of crops being grown, can be avoided through crop rotation. Furthermore, knowledge of the weeds which are in the same family as the crops being grown is important. These weeds can provide habitat for the same pests and diseases which will attack your vegetables. For instance, jimsonweed and black nightshade are both in the *Solanaceae* family. If potatoes are being grown nearby, these weeds can spread diseases and or pests. As a result, it is imperative to monitor and remove the growth of weeds around the area where you are growing food.

The Importance of Using Mulch

Another universal practice of growing food no matter where you live, what or how you are growing is to use mulch around your plants. Just as there are different types of mulches to use, there are multiple advantages of using mulch. One of the most important maxims of growing food is to reduce soil erosion by using mulch. Also, mulching significantly conserves soil moisture, reducing the amount of time needed to water the plants while decreasing the chances the plants will experience drought stress. The soil around plants which are not mulched usually dries up within a few hours, especially during a hot summer day. Often, I have noticed the soil around mulched plants is still moist even up to a week or longer since the last rain or watering. Numerous times during the growing season, I have been able to leave my crops unattended and go on vacation for a few days without worrying about them drying out. People always comment I am the only farmer who goes on vacation during the growing season and I attribute this to using mulch! Additionally, mulch helps to regulate soil temperatures during the growing season, thus providing more favorable conditions for plant growth. However, try not to apply heavy mulch in early spring when the soil temperature is colder, because the mulch can prevent the soil from warming to its desired temperature. Luckily, darker mulches can help increase the soil temperature during the beginning and end of the growing season when weather conditions are colder.

Another advantage of mulch is that it covers the bare soil which reduces the possibility of diseases. Various types of destructive diseases reside in the soil and spread more easily when the soil is not covered. These diseases can be displaced by the wind and carried through the air. Also, the diseases can be splashed by raindrops from the soil to the plant. For instance, septoria leaf spot, bacterial speck and blights are just a few of diseases spread from water droplets displacing these infected spores from bare soil to the leaves of the plants.[1] Once again, mulching is another of the many simple and natural methods which can prevent numerous avoidable problems with diseases and pests.

Fortunately, mulching helps to reduce the growth of weeds and lowers the amount of time you have to spend tending to your garden. When applied thick and immediately after planting, mulch helps to block the sunlight from activating weed seeds in the soil preventing them from growing. Weeding is often one of the most unfavorable and time-consuming activities for those who grow food. If left unchecked, weeds can rapidly inundate the plants to the point where an individual might give up the garden instead of spending the time and effort at removing the weeds. Weeds compete with plants for sunlight, water, air, and nutrients and can also provide habitat and food for pests and diseases. It is easier to monitor your plants for diseases and pests if they are grown in a clean, organized, weed-free and neatly mulched environment. If crops have more space around them, then the leaves and other plant parts will dry faster, reducing the outbreak of diseases. Luckily, mulching is so effective at controlling weeds that you will be amazed at how little time you will have to spend weeding. Mulching is better than the old-fashioned method of weed control on non-mulched ground using hoes and cultivators. Remember, this soil distrurbance reduces the health of the soil by increasing the rate of organic decomposition and by disturbing the earthworms and micro-organisms in the soil.

What types of mulch can one use? Black plastic, compost, hay, lawn clippings, leaves, newspapers, pine needles, sawdust, straw, and woodchips are common mulches. One of the greatest advantages of black plastic is its ability to warm the soil more than other mulches in the colder parts of the growing season. Since black plastic is not an organic mulch, it does not improve the structure of the soil by adding nutrients, organic matter and providing food for micro-organisms. However, if you are growing food in a large area, black plastic may be more efficient since it takes less time to apply than organic mulches. In recent years they have even developed biodegradable black plastic using materials such as corn. If you intend to use black plastic, make sure to wet the soil before applying and also to set up a drip irrigation system underneath the plastic since rainwater is less likely to get under the plastic. The major disadvantage of black plastic is it often makes a mess once it starts to break down and can get tangled in your equipment like the garden tiller.

Organic Mulches

Though organic mulches may take longer to spread than inorganic mulch, the extra effort is worth it since organic mulches have such positive soil building properties. Remember compost has benefits when added to the soil but an overuse of compost can result in excessive levels of phosphorous which can cause eutrophication. Also, I have noticed though it is weed free at first, if you use it as mulch on the soil surface, weeds will eventually grow faster compared to other mulches. Thus, when I use compost, I tend to only use a handful or two of compost around the base of plants and then I add mulch like straw on top.

One of the cheapest and easily accessible mulches is hay. Hay should be applied four to six inches in order to prevent weeds from growing. The one disadvantage of hay is that it usually contains high levels of weed seeds which can eventually germinate in the soil. The worst part about hay is it can also contain brambles and thorns which are a nuisance if you enjoy being barefoot in the garden. Though usually more expensive than hay, straw is another valuable mulch to use. To save costs, try to buy straw directly from farmers rather than from nurseries or hardware stores. Since straw tends to have far less weeds than hay, it helps to reduce weed growth around the plants. If you enjoy gardening barefoot, straw is more pleasing to the feet than the brambles and thorns found in hay. Straw should be applied four to six inches thick. Ever since I began using straw, it has now become my favorite mulch to use since it spreads easily, adds organic matter to the soil, looks pretty, smells like the earth, is effective and is comfortable to walk on barefoot.

Moreover, grass clippings are another easy to find and accessible mulch. Grass clippings tend to have higher levels of nitrogen which will decompose and enter the soil rapidly, thus helping to fertilize the plants. Also, I have noticed more earthworm activity around the areas where grass clippings are used in the garden. Grass clippings should be applied three to six inches thick and will probably have to be re-applied throughout the season since the grass tends to decompose faster than other mulches. What about grass clippings from lawns treated with herbicides, fungicides and insecticides? If you are concerned about directly applying them, then through the compost process, any toxins should be eradicated, and the finished product should be safe to use.

In the fall leaves are an easy to acquire mulch, especially when people rake leaves and place them in garbage bags or bins alongside the road. Ideally, to prevent nitrogen immobilization, you should allow the leaves to begin to decompose before adding them to the soil since they have a high carbon to nitrogen ratio. The best way to do this is to fence off an area with chicken fencing and pile the leaves atop one another. Then by the following year, this "leaf litter" can be used as an effective soil enhancing mulch which should be applied three to six inches thick. Just like the grass clippings, you will notice a great deal of earthworm activity in areas where you apply leaf litter. Additionally, non-colored newspapers can also be used as mulch and should be applied a few inches. Some suggest not using colored newspapers and magazines since they may contain lead and other chemicals. I have had the most success applying newspapers followed by another layer of mulch such as grass clippings. It is important to cover and secure the newspapers since they will otherwise blow away and create a mess. The greatest disadvantage of using newspapers is they tend to take the longest time to spread.

For acidic preferring plants like blueberry bushes, pine needles are often recommended to use as mulch. Some people claim that pine needles acidify the soil while others say that is not true since by the time they decompose they are in a neutral state. If using pine needles, apply three to six inches deep. A disadvantage of raking and using pine needles is that they often contain weed seeds such as morning glory. Another mulch for acidic preferring plants is sawdust. Though you must make sure to use sawdust from untreated wood. It should be applied just a few inches thick. Sawdust is much denser than other materials and blocks sunlight from activating weed growth more effectively.

Of all the mulches, the densest and thickest are woodchips. Woodchips are usually the longest lasting of the organic mulches since they take years to decompose. Thus, applying them three to six inches deep should last for an extended amount of time. I obtain woodchips in bulk from a local tree cutting service. Some people suggest that water does not infiltrate the soil as easily when woodchips are used as mulch. However, in my experience, I have not noticed this problem and am amazed just how wet the soil remains under woodchips. Just like grass clippings, I have noticed numerous earthworms living around the soil of the woodchips. Remember that sometimes when high carbon materials like woodchips are added to the soil it can cause nitrogen immobilization. Therefore, it is a great idea to apply some material high in nitrogen like glass clippings or synthetic nitrogen fertilizer before adding mulches high in carbon like woodchips, sawdust, newspapers, stray, leaves and hay to the soil.

Of all of the recommendations I give to people about growing food, using mulch is by far one of the most important. Mulching will conserve time by helping to control weeds and maintaining soil moisture, while enhancing organic matter, nutrients, and the structure of the soil.

Succession Planting

Another universal practice for growing food is to plant in succession. For instance, if you plant all your potatoes at once in the beginning of the season, then you will be harvesting all of your potatoes at once later in the season. This means you will have a great deal of planting and harvesting to do at the same time. A trick to enjoy growing food is to reduce the amount of work you have to do at one time. Moreover, if everything is harvested together, usually food will be thrown out since it is often too time consuming to eat or preserve everything. Furthermore, concerning long term storing crops like potatoes, you want to plan your planting date so that you have a final harvest at the end of the season. This will help you have plenty of potatoes to last throughout the winter and into the next spring. I often made the mistake of planting everything at once early in the season. Thus, the potatoes I planted in May and harvested in August/September, only lasted until December or January. Now since I plant potatoes in May and one last time in late June/early July, I enjoy an early season harvest and a late season harvest, which stores throughout the winter and often into until the spring.

Therefore, you want to be mindful of the first date which you can plant a crop, the days it takes to harvest, and the last expected frost of the season. Then you want to schedule your successive plantings so that you will not have one large harvest but rather multiple harvests extended throughout the season. This will make eating, canning, and preserving your food much more enjoyable and efficient. For example, if the first day to plant beans is after the frost has passed, which in my section of Pennsylvania is June 1st, and beans take 70 to 90 days to harvest, then the first harvest will be sometime in August. Imagine if you planted all your rows of beans at once and now in mid-August you have to either eat and or preserve all these beans! Unfortunately, I made this mistake multiple times my first few years of growing food. As a result, so much of what I grew was wasted, since I could not eat it all at once and since I did not know how to can and preserve food back then. However, if you plant a few plants or one row at a time, then wait another week to two weeks to plant the next row, you will enjoy small, successive harvests throughout the growing season. A wonderful idea is to write down the date you planted everything and the days it takes to harvest so you can have a general idea of when it should be mature and ready to harvest. Succession planting is another method of gardening independent of where you live or what or how you are growing, that will make your gardening experience more enjoyable.

From crop rotation, plant families, mulching, and succession planting, in addition to the aforementioned knowledge you have acquired from the first chapters, congratulations because you are now ready to begin growing food!

Chapter 4: Planting Vegetables

When is the growing season, when can you plant? Crops are classified as cool weather and warm weather crops. For warm weather crops like tomatoes, cucumbers, and peppers, these can be planted in the ground after the last expected frost of spring (June 1st in my neck of the woods). To determine when this is in your area, ask local growers and check out government maps like the USDA Hardiness Zone Map. Often, warm weather crops like peppers and tomatoes are grown indoors as transplants for a few weeks before the last frost to give them a head start. Otherwise, if you plant them from seed in the ground there will not be enough time during the growing season for them to produce vegetables. One can either start these transplants themselves or another method is to buy them from a local nursery.

The advantage of starting transplants yourself is that you can choose seeds from a wider variety than what is usually offered at nurseries. Moreover, there is the satisfaction of starting the plant from seed and watching it grow throughout its entire life cycle. When you finally eat the food you planted, as you taste the food in your mouth, you can visualize and remember the time and labor you invested all the way back to when you planted the first seed. This transcendental experience is what invokes a sense of gratitude, making one feel more alive, happy and healthy. All of a sudden, this is no longer just a meal, but an uplifting experience which forever enhances your perspective and feeling about this wonderful life we get to live.

Fortunately, if your time is limited like it is for me because I am busy with other outdoor work, buying transplants from nurseries is very convenient and affordable. Currently, I spend about $15 to $18 dollars for a full tray (often 18 to 30 plants) of transplants. Another money saving trick I learned, is that nurseries will sell their transplants at discount prices a few weeks after the last frost since most people stop buying the plants by then. However, there will obviously be less selection and some of these plants will be root-bound and show signs of stress. With some extra love and care, the latter bought transplants will become very productive. Thus, I usually buy the majority of transplants of summer annuals in the middle and end of May followed in a few weeks with the cheaper transplants. This way I get to plant in succession insuring a staggered harvest while saving money. If you want to make sure to get the best selection, then go a week or two before the last expected frost. This does not mean you have to plant them outdoors right away but rather you can care for them until it is safe to plant. Going a week or two before everyone else will help you avoid the frantic rush and long lines at nurseries. I find the best time to go to nurseries is on a weekday morning rather than on the weekends when it is very busy.

Concerning the cool weather crops, there is a time frame they can be planted in the weeks before the last frost of spring. For instance, onions can be planted four to six weeks beforehand. Since June 1st is the last frost date in my neck of the woods, I can plant onions in mid-April. Then like I said, I will plant in succession and sow another few rows in the following weeks. Just make sure the final planting gives enough time for the onions to grow and mature before they are killed by the freezing weather of late autumn. This way I can enjoy an early harvest and a latter harvest, which should provide onions in storage throughout the winter months and on into the spring.

How to Grow Onions

Like onions, the other members of the *Alliaceae* family including chives, garlic, leeks, and shallots, prefer the pH to be between 6.2 and 6.8 and have similar growing requirements. Onions enjoy being grown in rich, fertile soil with a sufficient amount of organic material. That is why it is recommended to apply a ¼ inch layer of compost or well rotted manure on top of the row where you are planting the onion. If you want to use chemical fertilizer, apply 4 ½ lbs of 5-10-10 fertilizer in low potash areas or 4 ½ lbs of 5-10-5 where potash levels are higher per 100 sq. feet.[1] Before planting, as with all fertilizers, it is advised to incorporate this fertilizer into the bulk of the soil profile. Thus, after adding my layer of fertilizer, I re-cultivate the row one or two more times with my tiller and then plant.

A common method of obtaining onions (*Allium cepa L.*) for planting is to buy them as immature, tiny bulbs called onion sets. When planting onions, make sure to place the flat part (where the roots will form) down about a half an inch into the soil. Plant the sets

1 ½ to 2 inches apart in rows which are about a foot apart. Then as the onions grow, thin to 4 inches apart. The advantage of this is that you can use the young tender plants you pull for immediate eating as scrumptious scallions! Within just a few weeks after planting, you can enjoy your first harvest of scallions in May and throughout the growing season. Taking some fresh scallions and cutting them up into smaller pieces and adding them to something basic like eggs can turn that food into a gourmet meal! Usually each day during the growing season, I will eat a fresh scallion or two. Being able to go outside and harvest them fresh will make all sorts of foods taste absolutely delicious.

If planting onions in the already growing plant form, place them 4 inches apart. Onions which are already growing should be harvested 30 to 40 days earlier than those which are planted as bulbs directly in the ground. Supposedly, onions started from bulbs take 80 to 110 days to harvest where those started as plants take 50 to 60 days to harvest. I planted both types thinking the onions plants would be ready earlier in the season. However, I was very surprised since the onion bulbs grew faster and bigger than the transplants! Therefore, from now on I am only going to plant onion bulbs. The onion bulbs are easier to work with and plant rather than trying to separate all the individual onion transplants which are grown together in tight plastic containers. It was time consuming to try to carefully untangle the roots from each plant and multiple plants died from transplant shock. Overall, it took less time to plant the bulbs than the onion plants.

Regardless of how you start your onions, there should be at least a foot of space between the rows. Therefore, with my garden tiller, I usually make a row that is about 18 inches wide. Then I place straw 4 inches tall along the middle of this row and plant the onions along both sides of the straw. If you take the straw directly from the bale and keep it square, the straw is usually wide enough for a foot of spacing between the rows. Concerning mulching, I find that it is easiest to lay down a row of straw before even planting the onions. This way, I can plant the onions against the row of straw. Countless times when I planted the onions first and then mulched, I accidentally covered the onions since I did not know where was the row. Now with this new method, once the row is mulched, I can plant the onions along both sides of this straw. Then, once the onions are in the ground, I add mulch to cover up the other side of the row. In the past I have used newspapers covered with grass clippings as mulch around onions. This is very labor intensive and takes a great deal of time so now I prefer using straw.

Six weeks after planting, the onions should be side dressed with different fertilizers depending on the use of the onion. For instance, for mild preferred tastings onions such as those used in salads, 1 lb of 5-10-10 fertilizer which does not contain sulfur should be applied per 200 ft of row about 3 inches away from the onions.[1] For more powerful onion flavor or for onions intended for long term storage, ¼ lb of ammonium sulfate should be placed per 100 ft of row about 3 inches away from the onions.[1] What if you do not know how much square feet of row you have? What if you have less than the recommended rate calls for? I simply lightly sprinkle some fertilizer around the plants. With trial and error, you will eventually understand how much fertilizer to use. The important thing is to not overuse the fertilizer. Remember if you intend to have onions for long term winter storage, time the last planting so there is enough time for the onions to mature so that they will be harvested as late in the season as possible.

An important thing to remember while growing onions is not to let the onion flower. When an onion flowers, it means the plant believes it is coming to the end of its life cycle. Thus, the onion bulb will not grow as large as if you were to remove the flower. This was another aspect of growing food which I learned from trial and error. The removal of the flower of a crop depends on the crop itself; so do not remove the flowers from the plant until you know the purpose of the flower. For instance, the flowers of pepper and tomato plants will eventually become the pepper or tomato. However, the flower of the onion becomes the seed. Onions are ready to harvest with the top part of the plant starts to fall over and turns yellow or brown. The upper plant part can be cut about an inch above the bulb. Make sure to allow the onions to dry indoors for a week or two before putting them in long term storage. Before storing them, I place them on a wire rack in a warm and sunny room to allow them to dry sufficiently.

Last year I learned a valuable lesson by not harvesting my onions in time. It is often recommended to harvest onions which are still growing around the time of the first heavy fall frost. However, I made the mistake of not harvesting them before the first fall freeze!

One night the temperatures unexpectedly dropped to the single digits and my remaining onions froze. If this happens, you have to use the onions immediately for making soups, broths, etc. Otherwise, the onions will start to rot. It is almost inevitable that you too will make mistakes while growing food. The true mistake occurs if you do not learn your lesson the first time. I can guarantee that from now on I will always harvest my onions on time.

For optimum storage, keep the onions in a cool (32 to 40 degrees F with 65% to 70% humidity) environment in a manner so that air can pass through them, such as in hanging mesh bags. Another trick for aeration and storage is to cut multiple holes in a brown paper bag with a hole puncher. People will say onions will store for only two to four months but I have had them store up to six months! When they are in storage for longer, they will start to grow from the inside. I simply remove the inner green growing part of the onion and get to enjoy another homegrown onion months after harvest. When it comes to food grown yourself, you are more likely to manicure the food and remove the bad parts since you have pride in the food. Often it is easier to discard food you bought from the store, since you do not have a personal connection with this food. Fortunately, growing your own food helps to reduce excess waste.

Health Benefits of Onions

According to the scientific journal Phytotherapy Research, "Compounds from onions have been reported to have anti-carcinogenic properties, anti-platelet properties (reduces heart disease), anti-thrombotic (reduces blood clots and stroke) properties, anti-asthmatic and anti-biotic effects".[2] The health benefits of onions can be partially attributed to the polyphenol quercetin.[2] Polyphenols (anti-oxidants) are plant compounds which give the plants their color.[3] Part of the function of the color is to help fight plant pathogens (diseases) and also to prevent damage from the sun's ultraviolet radiation.[3] Based on their structure, polyphenols (there are hundreds in edible plants) are further divided into different groups such as phenolic acids, flavonoids, and lignans.[3] These can be further divided into sub-groups such as catechins, proanthocyanidins, flavonols, and anthocyanidins.[3] While I will repeat these names throughout the book, and you may or may not remember them specifically, the important thing to remember is that they are anti-oxidants.

What Are Anti-Oxidants and Free Radicals?

What is the function and importance of anti-oxidants? Like other anti-oxidants, quercetin has been demonstrated to remove free radicals in the body's cells.[2] Therefore, this reduces excess oxidation and inflammation, the two main causes which disrupt normal cell functioning.[4] What are free radicals? According to the Harvard School of Health, free radicals are unpaired electrons within the body's cells which in order to become stable, will steal electrons from other parts of the cell such as proteins and DNA.[4] Ultimately, this causes a chain reaction of electron theft, which disrupts the normal functioning of the cell.[4] For instance, free radicals can change the shape of low density lipoproteins (LDL a.k.a. "bad cholesterol"), making them more likely to get trapped in the arteries, increasing the risk for heart disease.[4] Furthermore, free radicals can disrupt the normal instructions and coding of DNA, while also affecting the ebb and flow of what enters and leaves the cell.[4] Overall, by negatively affecting DNA, RNA, proteins and lipids within the cells, this substantially elevates the chances for autism, cancer, cardiovascular and other diseases.[5]

Where do free radicals come from? They are the result of everyday activities and metabolism, such as transforming food into energy, breathing, exercising, exposure to air pollution, and by unhealthy activities like cigarette smoking and chronic stress.[4] Free radicals belong to an essential group of molecules known as reactive oxygen/nitrogen species (ROS/RNS).[5] In smaller amounts, free radicals are responsible for normal functions of the cell such as apoptosis (programmed death of no-longer useful cells), cell signaling, gene expression and ion transportation.[5] However, an excess of free radicals is what disrupts normal cell functioning.[5] Luckily, anti-oxidants combat free radical damage by providing the free radicals with an unpaired electron, thus stabilizing the free-radical and preventing it from causing damage within the cell.[4]

The cardiovascular benefits of onions are the result of quercetin's ability to reduce low density lipoprotein oxidation, which helps prevent a buildup of plaque in the arteries.[6] Furthermore, the Zutphen Eldery Study demonstrated that elderly men with higher flavonoid (quercetin) intake especially from onions (also tea and apples) were less likely to experience coronary illness or death than men who consumed less flavonoids in their diet.[6] Who knew that onions which are used for everyday recipes and taste delicious contained so many powerful health benefits!

How to Grow Potatoes

Though potatoes (*Solanum tuberosum*) are often associated with European cultures, especially the Irish and Germans, they were originally domesticated and cultivated about 5,000 years ago in the Peruvian Andes Mountains in South America.[7] As aforementioned, potatoes are members of the *Solanaceae* family, including tomato, eggplant and pepper. Potatoes can start to be planted two to three weeks before the last expected frost. When planting potatoes, use certified seed potatoes and not potatoes from the grocery store. Certified seed potatoes have to pass an inspection for diseases and pests before being sold. This helps to insure you are starting off with healthy potatoes. Some people recommend not using potatoes which you stored from last year's crop since they can harbor insects and diseases. If you use them, make sure to treat them with copper and sulfur powder.

Unlike most vegetables, potatoes prefer a more acidic soil between 5.3 and 6.0. If you are unsure of the nutrient levels in the soil, use 2.5 to 3 lbs of 10-10-10 fertilizer per 100 feet of row.[1] Ideally, it is best to place the fertilizer 2 inches away from the potato in bands along the row, so it does not damage the young, tender growing potato. For compost or well rotted manure, add a ¼ layer to the soil then incorporate this into the bulk of the soil profile. Before actually planting the potatoes, it is a great idea to place them in a sunny room to allow the "eyes" to begin to form. These eyes will then grow a few inches before planting. Then, you can cut the seed potatoes into smaller pieces. Each one of these pieces should be the size of a small hen's egg or golf ball, with at least one or two eyes on the potato. Then, allow the cut pieces to dry for up to a week. This will seal the wounds which will prevent insects or diseases from easily attacking the potato seed once it is planted in the ground. Furthermore, I highly recommend dusting the potatoes with sulfur and copper powder before planting. The sulfur and copper powder helps prevent insects from eating the potato and also helps to lower the risk for diseases like potato blight. In trials I have done with and without this powder, I have noticed less problems with insects and diseases when the potatoes are treated with the powder. Mainly, the non-treated potatoes had higher incidence of wireworm damage. The wireworms burrow into the potato and eat it from the inside, causing the surrounding tissue to turn black. Even if you remove this section of the potato, it can still leave a very pungent and offensive taste throughout the rest of the potato. To add the sulfur and copper, I wet the potatoes in a bucket, remove them, and then thoroughly dust them with the powder. Before dusting, you can actually let the potatoes soak in the water bucket for a couple of hours so they have adequate water and are ready to grow as soon as you plant them. Last year, I did not bother to cut my potatoes into eyes, but rather I planted them whole. I attempted this method since it is suggested the potato has more energy and nutrition to put into growth if you do not cut the seed potato into smaller pieces. By trying this, I realized it saves time since you do not have to cut potatoes and let them dry for a week.

When planting, place the potatoes 3 inches deep with the growing eye facing up. If the eye is long enough, place it above the soil. Keep the potatoes 12 to 18 inches away from one another in rows 2 to 4 feet apart. From experience, I prefer to keep 4 feet between the rows of potatoes. Then as the potatoes grow, make sure to "hill" them by mounding up soil on all sides so that only perhaps no more than 8 inches of the potato plant is above the soil. When there is only 2 to 3 feet between the rows, there is usually not enough soil available to hill both rows. However, keeping 4 feet between rows allows sufficient spacing and insures there will be enough available soil to hill the potatoes.

Why is hilling potatoes important? If sunlight reaches the underground growing potatoes, it turns them green. This green portion is a poisonous alkaloid called solanine. Last winter, I accidentally ate this green section of the potato and suffered extreme abdominal pain and vomiting. Furthermore, hilling the potatoes also helps to keep them upright. This is important since if they are not hilled, they will bend over and break during stormy weather. When hilling potatoes, use this time to side dress the rows with fertilizer. I prefer to use 5-10-10 or 10-10-10 placed in bands a few inches from the plants. Afterwards, I mound the soil over the fertilizer and add another layer of straw over the bare soil. Through this method, the application of inorganic fertilizer will quickly provide nutrients for the potatoes. Also, the addition of mulch will add organic matter and nutrients to the soil while reducing soil erosion.

Potatoes usually take 100 to 120 days to harvest. From mid-May to late June/early July, I plant in succession. Since the July planted potatoes are harvested in late fall, they often keep in storage until the following spring. To insure a bountiful harvest, I highly suggest making sure to spray the potatoes. For instance, I use an insecticide by Bonide specifically for Colorado Potato Beetle (works on other pests and crops too) and sulfur based sprays to control fungal diseases like potato blight. While everything may seem to be growing well without sprays, all of a sudden one day you will be devastated at how much damage potato beetles can do overnight. In the beginning, I neglected to spray for bugs and blights. Sure enough my yields were reduced and in some instances, the bugs and blight killed the plants before they could even produce potatoes! As long as you maintain an active spray schedule from the time you plant the potatoes, you can avoid the devastation I experienced when I lost most of my crop to bugs and blight.

Potatoes are ready to harvest when the tops turn lighter brown and dry up. The light brown color of a ready to harvest potato is noticeably different than the dark, damp looking brownish/blackish color of potatoes infected with blight. For making cleaning off the potatoes easier, try to harvest them when there have been a few consecutive dry days. If you harvest them when the soil is wet, the potatoes will retain extra soil. Then when you go to wash them off before cooking, it will take longer and the sink will get full of soil. Luckily, if you harvest them after a few dry days, they are cleaner and easier to handle.

Make sure you allow the potatoes to dry indoors for a few days before storing them in a cool (35 to 40 degrees Fahrenheit), well aired place such as a root cellar. Do not dry the potatoes in a sunny location because being exposed to the sun for a short amount of time can turn the potatoes green. I accidentally did this once and had to cut off the skins of the potatoes every time I used them. For best storage, keep the potatoes in an aerated bin such as a milk crate. Also, periodically check your stored potatoes for ones which are beginning to rot and remove immediately. Otherwise, this spoilage can spread and further decay the rest of your potatoes.

Digging for Gold

Harvesting potatoes is one of my favorite aspects of growing food. When you dig up every plant, there is always a surprise! You never know if you are going to get any potatoes, how many you will get, and how big will they be! With each harvest of each plant, I find myself rejoicing and full of happiness. The harvest of potatoes seems to be more intimate than the other crops because you have to get down on your hands and knees, turn the soil over, and use your fingers to dig through the soil. The senses are truly saturated with the spirit of the soil. From the smells, to the feels, to the looks, and the taste, the whole process of growing and harvesting potatoes is transcendent, a renewal, a rebirth, a baptism by the earth! It is even better to harvest potatoes on a nice sunny day so you can soak up the rays of the sun and the strength of the soil.

To harvest the potatoes, place the potato digger (I've also used a pitchfork) a few inches away from the potato plant. Make sure the tines are going straight into the ground and not at an angle. Then, I step on the digger, force it into the ground a few inches and then wiggle it upwards. Next, I go to the other side, repeat this process and then I overturn the soil. Finally, I go through the soil with my hands to make sure I got all the potatoes.

During the winter months, there is nothing to warm the body and soul like taking some homegrown potatoes from the root cellar, cleaning off the lovely smelling soil that has dried on them, and cooking them into a delicious meal. Every time I use food during the winter that I grew in the summer, it brings back such fond memories of the summer and the intimate bond one has with the seasons when they are a participant in nature. So even on a cold, dark winter's day while most other people are complaining and depressed, you can feel so happy, grateful and connected all from the action of growing your own food.

Health Benefits of Potatoes

Potatoes include high levels of vitamins and minerals especially potassium and magnesium, a high level of fiber, and though they have less protein than other crops, the biological quality of the protein is actually almost as complete as an egg.[8] What exactly does this mean? Potatoes are easily digested and have sufficient levels of all twenty amino acids, especially the most limiting ones, lysine, methionine, threonine, and tryptophan.[8] Because potatoes contain a complete amino acid package, that means most of the proteins consumed in the potato and with the rest of the meal, will be digested and utilized by the body. Even if the foods you are eating are limiting in one amino acid, you will absorb less protein compared to a meal with all twenty amino acids. No wonder why growing up I often heard people say eat your potatoes if you want to get big!

The high amount of potassium in potatoes reduces blood pressure, the risk for stroke and cardio-vascular disease.[8] Moreover, though responsible for over 300 metabolic reactions in the body, about 60% of adults in the United States do not consume enough magnesium.[8] According to Dr. Connie Weaver of Purdue University:

> "It is this marginal to moderate magnesium deficiency, through aggravating chronic inflammatory stress that may be contributing significantly to the occurrence of atherosclerosis (plaque accumulation in the arteries), hypertension (high blood pressure) osteoporosis, type 2 diabetes, mellitus (diabetes), and certain types of cancer".[8]

Interestingly, this same report demonstrates that people, especially children, are more likely to eat more of the vegetables with their meal if they are combined with potatoes.[8] Potatoes make you strong and healthy and they taste delicious, a win-win situation for everyone.

Broccoli

In addition to potatoes, another tasty, refreshing and nutritious crop which can be planted two to three weeks before the last expected frost is broccoli (*Brassica oleracea*). Within rows, broccoli should be planted about 12 to 18 inches apart and about 3 feet apart between rows. Before planting, incorporate a ¼ inch of compost or well rotted manure on the soil surface. Or if you prefer synthetic fertilizer, use about 3 lbs of 5-10-10 fertilizer for every 100 square feet of row.[9] Especially with broccoli, it is important to add the trace elements boron and molybdenum to prevent brown and misshapen broccoli heads from forming.[10] Of course, make sure to incorporate the fertilizer into the soil profile rather than leaving it on the soil surface. Concerning the pH, broccoli prefers to be grown in soil with a 6.0 to 6.8 pH range. As always, make sure to immediately mulch the area around the broccoli after planting.

If left unchecked, slugs and other pests can have a devastating effect on your broccoli plants. One of the best ways to control slugs is by placing cups filled with ¼ of beer in the soil. The slugs will smell the yeast and think what a feast! Then when they fall into the cup, the slugs will not be able to get up. Through this method, I have literally found dozens of slugs in the cups overnight. This is by far the most efficient and cost effective method to control slugs. Additionally, you can go into the garden at night with a flashlight and drop the slugs into a cup of water with salt. As with other forms of pest control, it is essential to prevent an outbreak from occurring in the first place. Rather than waiting until you notice there is a problem in the middle of the season, make it a routine to place the cups of beer in the soil immediately after planting and to monitor and remove the slugs from the very beginning. Regarding sprays, I use a combination of Neem Oil, Cayenne Pepper Concentrate and dish detergent. When I am spraying my potatoes with the Bonide Colorado Potato Beetle spray, I also use it on the broccoli plants since it helps control insects like Cabbage Worms. I find using sulfur based sprays will also help reduces diseases. Overall, these various sprays do an excellent job controlling diseases and insects.

In order to enjoy a continuous harvest of broccoli throughout the season, I plant broccoli in succession every two weeks until the middle of July. The wonderful thing about broccoli is that when you harvest the first round, side shoots will develop a few more rounds of broccoli from each plant. To increase new shoots, I always make sure to cut the broccoli at an angle leaving a few tiny broccoli heads on the plant. These little heads will eventually grow into a large broccoli head.

It is essential to harvest the broccoli before it goes to flower. For optimum flavor, you must harvest the broccoli while the heads are still tight and green. When they start to open up and turn yellow, the flavor will change and they will soon flower. Just like onions, if the broccoli flowers the plant will produce less since it thinks it has completed its life cycle. A refreshing sensation is to pick and eat broccoli in the early morning while there is still dew on the leaves or after a rainstorm on a hot and humid summer day. Speaking of the morning, some claim this is the best time to harvest food since it is believed the taste is better rather than being picked during the heat of the day. Personally, I never noticed a difference. Overall, broccoli is by far one of the most refreshing and nourishing crops to eat from the garden.

Health Benefits of Broccoli

The most fascinating health benefits of broccoli are the effects of sulforaphane. This is a unique compound found in cruciferous vegetables like broccoli which has been suggested to reduce the risk of cardio-vascular diseases and cancer.[11] How does this happen? Recall that when there is an excess of oxidation in the body's cells, it accelerates the destruction of the cells (similar to how we learned an excess of oxidation in the soil causes decomposition of the organic matter). Too much oxidation results in prolonged inflammation of the cells which increases the risk for various diseases.[11] A study from The Journal of Agricultural and Food Chemistry indicated that sulforaphane did in fact reduce oxidation in cells.[11] This decreased the breakdown of the cell's DNA and increased the overall health of the cells.[11]

Furthermore, research from the Proceedings of the National Academy of Sciences of the United States (PNAS), revealed that sulforaphane helped to lower the risk for cancer.[12] In this study, they purposely applied cancer to in-vitro cells and then administered sulforaphane while some of the cells did not receive the sulforaphane.[12] The results indicated that the ability of the cancer cells to replicate was reduced, the formation of cancer cells was delayed and the weight of the cancer cells was lower than in the non-treated cells.[12] By growing and consuming more broccoli throughout your life, you will increase your intake of its heart healthy and anti-carcinogenic properties, which could prevent heart disease and cancer from forming in the first place.

How to Freeze Broccoli

Luckily you can enjoy homegrown broccoli beyond the growing season by freezing it. To freeze broccoli, the first step after harvesting is to wash it off. Next, blanch the broccoli in boiling water for 1 ½ minutes to 3 minutes. Multiple recipes say to do it for 3 minutes, though numerous chefs and other people told me 3 minutes is too long and 1 ½ minutes is sufficient. Overall, the point of blanching is to help the broccoli freeze better by destroying the enzymes and bacteria which otherwise would cause the broccoli to go bad in the freezer. After blanching in boiling water, add the broccoli to a container of cold water with ice cubes for a few minutes. This will rapidly cool the broccoli down preventing it from being overcooked. Then, allow the broccoli to dry as much as possible. To store it efficiently, I recommended the use of a vacuum powered sealer machine such as the brand name Food-Saver. This machine works wonders since it removes the air out of the bag, seals it with heat, and the bag itself is designed to prevent freezer burn. Costing about $100 dollars for the machine and the bags, this is definitely a worthwhile investment since it will help you enjoy your vegetables after the growing season. It also helps keep food fresher for longer versus using regular plastic freezer bags. From experience, I learned a valuable trick which will save you frustration and time; put the broccoli on a flat, cloth-covered tray and place it in the freezer for a few hours before using the Food-Saver. Otherwise, it is nearly impossible to get a proper seal on the bag if the contents you are trying to seal are still wet. However, when the remaining water on the broccoli is frozen, the Food-Saver works incredibly.

Tomatoes

There are several other cool weather crops which can be planted before the last expected spring frost. However, since I do not particularly enjoy eating these vegetables, I do not bother planting them. Now I am going to focus on the warm weather vegetable annuals which can be planted after the last expected frost (June 1st in my growing zone). My absolute favorite summer vegetable (or is it a fruit) to grow is tomatoes (*Solanum lycopersicum*). They are the one crop which I will never eat unless homegrown. Non-homegrown tomatoes are usually the most tasteless and unpalatable of all the crops. However, tomatoes picked fresh from the vine are one of the most appetizing, refreshing and energizing things to eat. My good friend old man Rayford recommends taking a salt shaker to the garden and sprinkling the tomatoes. Even when canned, the tomatoes are just as delicious if not better than fresh ones. Canned tomatoes are even tastier when they are opened and eaten on a cold winter's day, months after being harvested. You literally feel like you are opening a jar of summer sunshine, memories and vitality.

If starting from transplants, sow your tomato seeds indoors six to eight weeks before the last expected frosts. The optimum pH for tomatoes is between 6.0 and 6.5. Are you unsure of the fertility of the soil? Then apply a 1/4 inch layer of compost or well rotted manure and incorporate it into the soil before planting. Or if you prefer using chemical fertilizers and are unaware of the soil fertility, for every 100 sq. feet apply 3 lbs of 5-10-10.[13] In previous years if soil amendments high in potash like manure and compost have been utilized, use 5-10-5.

When using chemical fertilizer, it is important to make sure the fertilizer has lower levels of nitrogen and higher levels of potassium. Too much nitrogen for tomatoes will result in excessive vegetative growth and less fruit. Potassium is important for tomatoes since potassium helps to modify water levels in the fruit. Therefore, this will help to reduce problems with cracking and Blossom End Rot. At planting time, I usually add a tablespoon of fertilizer to the bottom of the planting hole mixed in with some soil. Then I add regular soil on top of that followed by the planting of the tomato. This method insures the roots will not come into contact with the fresh fertilizer preventing them from being burned. Another valuable soil amendment for tomatoes is to add a tablespoon of Epsom Salt to the planting hole and then thoroughly mix it with the soil. The Epsom Salt is composed of sulfur and magnesium which will help the tomato grow more rapidly and produce higher yields. Do you only have a few tomatoes to plant? Then I would use a tablespoon of fertilizer and Epsom Salt. Place them in the planting hole, and cover them up with an inch or two of soil. Just make sure the tomato roots do not immediately come into contact with the fertilizer. This method of using a tablespoon of fertilizer can also be used with most plants.

When planting, you can also incorporate organic soil amendments like compost or peat moss to improve the water holding capacity of the soil. Tomatoes are sensitive to changes in the water content availability of the soil. If they experience constant fluctuations throughout the season, then they will develop Blossom End Rot. This appears as black cracks on the surface which misshape the tomato, making it less appealing and appetizing. These cracks can serve as an entry point for diseases and pests. You can still eat a tomato with Blossom End Rot by removing the bad parts. To reduce the possibility of Blossom End Rot, I also add gypsum (calcium) to the soil. An organic option is to use bone meal and or egg shells. Mulching is important to keep the soil moist, reduce weeds and to prevent soil borne diseases. For example, Septoria Leaf Spot is caused when water droplets splash soil particles containing this disease to the lower leaves of the tomato plant. Using dark colored mulch or plastic for tomatoes will keep the soil warmer since the dark color helps absorb the sun's radiation. Personally, I enjoy using organic mulches like straw since it adds valuable organic matter to the soil. After properly amending the soil and mulching, the best way to prevent Blossom End Rot is to keep your tomatoes on a regular watering schedule.

Seasoning Transplants to Outdoor Conditions

As with all transplants, it is imperative to season the plants to outdoor growing conditions for up to a week before actually planting them. Transplants are accustomed to the easier growing conditions in greenhouses versus the outside world. In the greenhouse the sun and the wind are not as strong as outside. Thus, if a transplant is planted without being hardened, it can experience stress and die. Usually, they get sunburn and expire within a few hours. That is why it is essential to season the transplants in the following manner. First, place them outside for a few hours, preferably in the evening or morning while avoiding the harsh midday sun. Then for a few days, increase the amount of time each day the plants are exposed to outdoor conditions.

For all transplants, it is preferred to plant on a cloudy, rainy and calm day with rain or clouds in the upcoming forecast. The most important thing is to avoid planting on hot, sunny or windy days. Also, check the forecast to make sure there is not extreme hot or sunny weather in the few days following your transplanting date. As always, make sure to water your transplants. Even if the plants start to wilt, with water and care within a day or two they should resume their upright vigorous growing posture. While the ideal watering time is in the evening or early morning, I also water fresh planted transplants during the day since they are in a vulnerable stage. You can further protect your plants by covering them with a container like an old plant pot. Just make sure there are enough holes in the container so air can pass through and it does not trap heat. I also place a rock or stick around the base of the plant and then add the plant pot so that air can flow underneath. If some or all of your transplants die, do not worry and especially do not give up. Try again and you will win!

One of the tricks I learned with tomatoes is to plant the stalk a few inches below the soil because the little fibrous hairs of the tomato stalk will actually form roots underground. Planting it deeper will also make the tomato plant sturdier. Thus, if I have a twelve inch tomato transplant, I will place it a few inches deep in the soil, above the soil line of the original container it was grown in. Tomatoes are unique regarding this since with most plants or trees we want to plant them at the same soil level in which they were originally grown.

A few weeks after planting, once tiny tomatoes start to form, it is recommended to add a tablespoon of fertilizer to each plant. As usual, make sure to keep the fertilizer a few inches away from the base of the plant to prevent burning of the roots. Also, remember to always cover and incorporate the fertilizer into the soil so that it is not leached into the watershed or volatilized into the atmosphere by the sun. This side dressing of fertilizer can be repeated one or two more times during the growing season with at least three weeks between applications. After adding the fertilizer, slowly water the soil so the fertilizer begins to work.

There are two different common methods to grow tomatoes. The first is to allow the tomatoes to grow on the ground without being staked. For non-staked tomatoes, plant in rows 2 to 3 feet apart with 3 to 5 feet between the plants. This method allows for less maintenance and potentially more yield. It is absolutely essential to make sure to mulch these tomatoes with straw (or whatever you prefer). However, even when mulch like straw is used, I noticed the tomatoes are more susceptible to pest and rodent damage since the tomatoes are at ground level. Furthermore, many tomatoes grown this way end up rotting since the plant does not have the ability to air out compared to if it was staked. Because of the prolonged wet conditions of non-staked tomatoes, it increases the chances for the spread of fungal diseases.

For these reasons, I prefer to stake my tomatoes and allow them to grow upright on one or two main stems. Staked tomatoes should be planted in rows 3 to 4 feet apart with 15 to 24 inches between each plant within the rows. Make sure to use wooden or metal stakes which are at least 5 feet tall. Some people caution against metal stakes since they can get very hot, especially on sunny days with high temperatures. However, I have never had a problem with using metal stakes for tomatoes. As the tomato grows, tie the tomato plant to the stake using all sorts of things from string, twine, plant ties to panty hose. If you are growing dozens of tomato plants, you can place stakes every 5 to 10 feet and run a horizontal trellis to which the tomato plants can be tied. To reduce diseases, disinfect your stakes at the end and the beginning of the season.

With most crops, I tend to keep the spacing between the tomato plants and between rows on the higher end of the recommended rate. This makes working and walking around the plants easier and also prevents overcrowding. It is very important to train the tomatoes from the beginning to only allow one or two main stems. Moreover, you want to regularly remove "suckers", or the plant tissue which grows in between the forks of main branches. Make sure to stay on top of your tomato pruning before the parts you have to remove are large. Otherwise, when removed, this will take away valuable nutrients from the plant. Furthermore, the large open wounds will allow for a loss of water and serve as an entry point for diseases and pests. Also, if a large section of the plant is pruned and all of a sudden the tomatoes are exposed to an increase of sunlight, they will experience sunscald. My preferred method to stay on top of pruning is to set aside a time and a day each week, usually Sunday morning, to thoroughly inspect each tomato plant and to remove suckers. Furthermore, while you are pruning, remove any diseased sections of the plant and burn them or throw them away in the garbage. It is imperative to clean your pruning tools from plant to plant or you can spread diseases.

During the later part of the growing season, a valuable trick is to remove the newly forming flowers and sections of the plant which will not produce tomatoes by the time of the fall frost. This will allow the tomatoes which are not ripe yet to ripen faster. By the time of the fall frost, non-ripe tomatoes can be picked green and wrapped in newspaper to be placed in a dry, warm and dark room. The tomatoes will eventually ripen because the newspaper will trap the ethylene gas. In order to enjoy a bountiful tomato harvest, you must be proactive about controlling diseases and insects with a regular spray schedule. I use a combination of sulfur based sprays, Neem-Oil, Cayenne Pepper Concentrate and dish detergent. Once again, when using sprays for other crops like Bonide Colorado Potato Beetle, I will check the label and see if it can be used on tomatoes. Since this spray will control insects on tomatoes, I use it. They also make various sprays specifically for tomatoes. When using sprays, remember, it is about prevention rather than treatment. If you notice a problem and then decide to spray it can be too late. You must realize diseases and insect damage are inevitable so spray from the beginning of the season.

How to Can Tomatoes

For years, I did not even bother to learn how to can tomatoes since I thought the process was too difficult. However, once someone finally taught me, I was astonished at how easy is the process. If I can "can", than you can "can"! After harvesting some tasty tomatoes from the garden and washing them off, the first step is to blanch them in boiling water for about two minutes or until you notice that the skins are beginning to crack and peel. Then, place the tomatoes in ice cold water for a few minutes. Next, the skins should peel off easily. I noticed it is easier to peel the skins when they begin to crack during the boiling process rather than assuming they will crack after they are submerged in the ice water. Now is a great time to remove any diseased or unwanted parts like the tougher core. What size you want to cut the tomatoes is up to you. Before placing the tomatoes in the mason jar, make sure the jars are thoroughly washed in boiling water. You must bring the water to boil in order to kill all potential pathogens. Some suggest using the dishwasher is sufficient. Also, you can wash the rings in hot water and soap. However, do not wash the lids in excessively hot water since this can alter the adhesive substance, thus preventing the jars from sealing properly during the canning process. Therefore, it is recommended to clean the lids in distilled white vinegar followed by rinsing in warm running water before being used.

It is imperative to make sure the jars do not have any cracks in them. While the jars and rings can be reused, the lids must be new each and every time. As you are filling the jar, use a disinfected flat plastic spatula to go up and down along the edges making sure there are no air pockets inside. Do not use a metal utensil such as a butter knife, since the metal can spoil the canning process because of oxidation. For canning salt, add a teaspoon for pint jars or two teaspoons per quart jars. Fill the jars with tomatoes up to ½ inch from the top of the jar. Then, make sure to wipe the top part of the jar with a clean cloth so there is absolutely no tomato or juice in this area. Otherwise, this can prevent a tight seal from occurring when you place the jars in the pressure canner. When placing the lid on the jar, make sure it is tight enough but not over-tightened. I usually turn it enough with my hand until it stops turning. Do not force it past this point because then it will be highly unlikely the canning process will work. If it is too tight, then the air from inside of the jar will not be able to escape and form a proper seal during the canning process.

Before placing in the pressure canner, add enough warm water to the canner so the water comes up ¼ of the way to the jars. I use the Power Pressure Cooker for canning instead of the old fashioned canners. How much time should tomatoes be canned? Most canners come with a booklet on this information but generally it is for ten to twenty minutes. Again this varies based on the person. Some people tell me ten minutes is sufficient while others say twenty is better. I also heard that canning them for longer will help them last longer in storage. As usual, make sure to follow all directions and if possible, it definitely helps to have someone who has canned before to help you out. To make canning easier, harvest your ripe tomatoes once or twice a week and do a little at a time. Do not wait until you have a bountiful harvest to try to can all the tomatoes. You will not enjoy the process if you have to do too much work at once. Rather, if you take an hour or two out of the day once or twice a week to can, by the end of the season you will have enjoyably canned dozens of jars.

Health Benefits of Tomatoes

According to The Journal of Pharmacognosy and Phytochemistry:

"Tomatoes can make people healthier and decrease the risk of conditions such as cancer, osteoporosis and cardiovascular disease. People who eat tomatoes regularly have a reduced risk of contracting cancer diseases such as lung, prostate, stomach, cervical, breast, oral, colorectal, esophageal, pancreatic, and many other types of cancer".[14]

What exactly is in tomatoes that give them such powerful health properties? Tomatoes contain all four major carotenoids, the phytochemical properties (polyphenols) of a fruit or vegetable which give them their color.[14] The red color of the tomato is from the carotenoid lycopene, which is one of the most powerful anti-oxidants.[14] As reported by The Journal of The National Cancer Institute, among 72 studies on the relationship between tomatoes, lycopene and cancer, 57 of these studies demonstrated higher intake of tomatoes and lycopene decreased the risk for cancer.[15] While lycopene is very healthy for you, only a few foods like tomatoes (then watermelon, grapefruit, and apricots) have high levels of it.[15]

Furthermore, tomatoes lower bad cholesterol levels (LDL or Low Density Lipoprotein) and blood pressure because of the effects of the anti-oxidants beta-carotene, Vitamin E, Vitamin C, Vitamin B and potassium.[14] Additionally, tomatoes reduce blood pressure because they contain a significant amount of gamma amino butyric acid (GABA).[14] Tomatoes also improve cardiovascular health since the Vitamin B6 and folate reduce the ability of a chemical called homocysteine to damage blood vessel walls.[14] Concerning diabetes, a study from the American Diabetes Association demonstrated tomatoes help diabetics regulate their blood sugar levels more effectively because of substantial levels of a trace element known as chromium.[16] There are countless more documented health benefits of tomatoes that perhaps a whole book could be written about it!

Peppers

Peppers (*Capsicum*) are one of the most rewarding and productive plants to grow. Preferring the pH to be between 6.2 and 6.8, peppers should be planted about 18 inches apart in rows and 2 to 3 feet apart between rows. To increase yields, it is advised to make sure the peppers are planted close enough so the leaves of the different plants actually come into contact with one another once the plants are mature. If you intend to grow peppers from seed, then you must start them indoors eight to ten weeks before the last expected frost of spring. As with all other transplants, make sure to gradually expose and acclimate the plants to outdoor conditions in the week before planting. When planting peppers, an organic fertilizer option is to add about a ¼ inch of compost or well rotted manure to the soil which should then be incorporated into the bulk of the soil profile.

If your nutrient levels are unknown, concerning chemical fertilizers, add 3 ½ lbs of 5-10-5 fertilizer and 1 lb of a phosphate based fertilizer like bone meal per every 100 sq feet.[1] At the onset of fruit development, a side dressing of chemical fertilizer like 10-10-10 is recommended. As with all fertilizer applications, try to cover the fertilizer with soil and or mulch. Once again, make sure to add mulch like straw around your pepper plants. One of the main problems I have had with peppers is the soil has been too wet. I learned a valuable lesson not to add too much compost, organic matter and or peat moss in the planting hole since this keeps the roots excessively wet. When the roots are too saturated, they do not grow efficiently and the rest of the plant is adversely affected. One of the symptoms of wet roots is that the pepper plant suffers from Phytophthora Blight. As a result, the leaves and fruit of the pepper become brown or black and the peppers become unpalatable. To avoid these wet soil conditions, try not to water every day, but rather every few days. Also, by not constantly applying water, the roots will be encouraged to grow more in their search for water.

Additionally, another mistake I made planting peppers was to not stake them. Towards the middle and end of the season when the pepper plants are loaded with peppers, high winds and rain can cause limbs and or the entire plant to break. However, if the plant is tied to a stake then this problem can be avoided. As with staking any plant or tree, make sure to do it at planting time to avoid injuring the roots. When it comes to harvesting peppers, carefully cut the pepper off the plant using a knife or scissors. If you use your hand and try to take the pepper, you can tear and rip off other parts of the plant. Interestingly, when there is a frost coming and you still have peppers on the plant, you can dig up the plant and hang it upside down indoors next to a sunny window and the non-ripe peppers will start to mature.

Freezing Peppers

When it comes to long-term pepper storage, freezing them without blanching them is the worst method. When you thaw non-blanched peppers, they taste awful and are mushy. If you are going to freeze them, you must blanch them in boiling water for two minutes if they are sliced and three minutes if the peppers are whole. Then, submerge them in a container of cold water with ice cubes for a few minutes. Afterwards, I place the peppers on a flat, cloth-covered tray in the freezer for a few hours so it is easier to use the FoodSaver machine. Next, I cut my FoodSaver freezer bags to the desired length and then seal the peppers using the FoodSaver. Peppers frozen properly taste absolutely delicious. I enjoy using them in omelettes, cheese-steaks, and to sauté them in first cold pressed olive oil, grass fed butter, canned tomatoes, and homegrown onions.

Health Benefits of Peppers

Peppers are similar to tomatoes with how they have multiple types of carotenoids and thus contain the varying health benefits of these powerful anti-oxidants. Specifically, the high level of the anti-oxidant Vitamin E in peppers has been demonstrated to combat dementia.[17] According to the Journal of the American Medical Association, "We found that higher dietary intake of vitamin E, but not vitamin C, beta carotene, or flavonoids, was associated with lower long-term risk of dementia over a mean of 9.6 years in the Rotterdam Study".[17] How does this happen? The authors explain how Vitamin E's anti-oxidative properties help to mitigate the destructive effects of β-amyloid, a major amino-acid that causes the accumulation of plaque in the brain which is responsible for dementia.[17] Throughout life, as β-amyloid is active in the brain, it causes inflammation which destroys healthy brain cells and increases the risk for dementia.[17] Fortunately, if you expose yourself daily to a healthy lifestyle including high consumption of fruits and vegetables like peppers, the properties of the anti-oxidants can potentially prevent devastating diseases like cancer, heart disease and dementia from forming in the first place!

Cucumbers

Finally, the last summer vegetable I enjoy growing are cucumbers (*Cucumis sativus*). A member of the *Cucurbitacea* or the "gourd" family, including squash, pumpkins and zucchini, these vegetables prefer the pH to be between 6.2 to 6.8. If you are unsure of the fertility levels, use 3 1/2 lbs of 5-10-5 fertilizer (use only 1 1/2 lb for watermelon) with a supplemental lb of phosphate such as steamed bone meal for every 100 square feet of the growing area.[1] Since members of the gourd family thrive in soils with high organic matter, incorporate compost and or peat into the planting hole with an additional ¼ layer on the soil surface around the base of each plant.

Spreading outwards in all directions, it is important to give cucumbers (and other gourds) plenty of space. For example, I usually leave about 6 to 8 feet of space between rows, though most people recommend only 5 feet. Within the rows themselves, I space the plants about 4 feet apart, though others suggest anywhere from 6 inches to 4 feet. I enjoy the extra spacing since it usually makes it easier to walk and work around the cucumbers. Instead of one plant per section, I actually place 2 or 3 plants together. With cucumbers, I practice another type of conservation tillage known as "no-till". About one week before planting, I spray an herbicide to kill the vegetation (you can also use dark tarps). Then instead of cultivating all the soil or even doing zone tilling, I just use a shovel to dig my planting holes every few feet. This method is valuable and practical for members of the gourd family since they are planted farther apart and will end up spreading in all directions.

Another valuable trick is that cucumbers and other gourds benefit from the addition of Epsom salts which makes them taste sweeter. I usually add a tablespoon to each planting hole or per every 100 square feet of planting area, add 3 lbs of Epsom salt.[1] Since magnesium is important for cucumbers, make sure to use dolomitic limestone (contains magnesium and calcium) when it comes time to lime the soil. Concerning mulching, black mulches are recommended for members of the gourd family since they help to warm the soil. Since I prefer organic mulches, I use straw. Using an herbicide before planting with the addition of mulch at planting are effective measures to control weeds. To control insects and diseases, I use Neem-Oil, Cayenne Pepper Concentrate, dish detergent and sulfur based sprays. Again, I will use sprays meant for other crops if the label says they can also be used on cucumbers. I make it a habit of spraying all of my crops together to better control insects and diseases. The main issues with cucumbers are from aphids. Since they are so small and hide on the underside of the leaves, they can go undetected. Then one day, your cucumber plants will start to wilt up and die from the aphids puncturing the plant's tissues. This causes dehydration of the plant while simultaneously spreading diseases. Regarding diseases, as the season progresses, Powdery Mildew becomes a serious problem. This is caused by poor circulation and constantly wet leaves. Since I keep my cucumbers well spaced, mulched and I only water at the base of the plant, I am doing everything to prevent this disease. I noticed around early August, the nights begin to get more dew. This daily dew coverage is what causes Powdery Mildew on my cucumbers. Luckily, as long as you spray on a regular basis from the beginning of the season, this should prevent pests and diseases from being a problem.

Health Benefits of Cucumbers

One of the most unique and significant properties of cucumbers is that they contain the flavonol (a phytochemical) fisetin.[17] The anti-oxidative and anti-inflammatory properties of fisetin have been suggested to reduce the risk for Alzheimer's Disease (AD) and various cancers.[17] Concerning Alzheimer's Disease, The Anatomical Society indicated that oral administration of fisetin to mice with AD significantly improved their memory and cognitive ability versus mice with AD who were not administered fisetin.[17] As previously mentioned, researchers believe AD is caused by decades of chronic inflammation in the brain which causes cell degeneration. Luckily for those of us who enjoy cucumbers, this same report demonstrated fisetin reduced multiple causes of neuroinflammation and neurodegeneration.[18]

How do cucumbers combat cancer? According to a study from Biochemical Pharmacology, the fisetin in cucumbers helps to fight melanoma and pancreatic cancers by inhibiting two pathways, PI3K/Akt and the mTOR.[19] These eventually lead to the formation of tumors.[19] The authors conclude by stating, "Our observations and findings from other laboratories suggest that fisetin could be a useful chemotherapeutic agent that could be used either alone or as an adjuvant with conventional chemotherapeutic drugs for the management of prostate and other cancers".[19] Incredible! So now while you are eating your cucumbers and enjoying the cool and refreshing sensations that soothe the body on a hot summer's day, you can think about how this cucumber is helping to prevent cancer and Alzheimer's disease!

While I have shared my personal knowledge and experience I have acquired from growing vegetables, in addition to the science behind it, the best way for you to learn is to go out there and do it yourself.　Do not be afraid of making mistakes for they are a wonderful opportunity to learn and to grow.

Chapter 5: How to Grow Blueberries and Raspberries

One of the greatest advantages of planting fruit like blueberries (*Vaccinium*) is that they are perennials and will come back every year. Therefore, it is a critical investment to improve the soil for a year or two before you even plant. Whether you intend to plant a dozen or 200 blueberry bushes, it is imperative to follow pre-planting procedures. For instance, adjusting soil pH and nutrient levels, using cover crops and establishing a relatively weed free growing area by planting perennial grasses like fescue and rye are important. Though you may be super excited and eager to plant fruit immediately, if you neglect pre-planting procedures, it is likely you will encounter various problems which you will have to deal with for many years. Since fruit bushes/trees can last decades, implementing the following preliminary procedures will improve production and decrease the amount of time, labor and money needed to maintain what you plant.

Blueberries

Blueberries are a productive, nutritious, and delicious fruit that do not take up too much space and can easily be accommodated into the landscape. If you decide to buy a dozen blueberry bushes and plant them in the corner of your yard, chances are you will be just one of the many people who struggle to grow blueberries. While I am busy picking pounds and pounds of berries to make wine, pancakes, pies, and more, you will be lucky to get just a handful of berries a year. Luckily, you are smart enough to apply the following steps before you even plant your blueberry bushes

Site Selection

Concerning site selection, the requirements are similar to vegetables including: a well drained location, protection from excessive wind, but an area that receives enough wind flow to dry wet leaves and fruit and to reduce the risk of frost damage, far enough away from competing trees, and an area which gets sunlight for ideally ¾ per day, with at least a minimum of six hours of direct sunlight. What is the best soil type for blueberries? According to the *Mid-Atlantic Berry Guide for Commercial Growers*, while berries grow the best in sandy loam soils high in organic matter, improving the organic matter content of the soil to 2% up to an optimum level of 5% will enhance production even in clay soils.[1] Why are clay soils undesirable for growing blueberries? Blueberries grow poorly in clay soils since their tiny roots have a hard time infiltrating through the dense and tightly held together clay soil particles. Thus, the roots have a more difficult time accessing both water and nutrients in clay soils. Luckily, you can address what are normally unsuitable growing soils for blueberries by removing ¼ of the original soil from the planting hole. Then, replace it with peat and mix it thoroughly with the remaining original soil. Often people have the misconception that blueberries like to be planted in wet soils because they are accustomed to seeing wild blueberries along the edges of lakes or ponds. However, these berry bushes are not growing directly in the water. Avoid planting blueberries in excessively wet soils since they will experience root rot like Phytophthora and will grow poorly if they even survive.[2]

Of course blueberries need water so the ideal situation is to have the soil moist but not saturated. Since blueberries have shallow roots, keeping the blueberry rows mulched with up to four to six inches of organic mulches will improve the growing conditions. For example, sawdust wood chips, and pine needles (Douglas Fir is the most recommended), are wonderful mulches to utilize. In addition to mulching, make sure to have easy access to water just in case you have to irrigate your blueberries especially during periods of drought. Fortunately, in the years I have been growing blueberry bushes, even during droughts, the thick four to six inch layer of organic mulch has been sufficient to keep the soil moist enough for the blueberries to survive the dry weather. Also, mulching is important since it will reduce weeds and add valuable nutrients to the soil, feeding both the blueberries and soil micro-organisms. Additionally, mulch will acidify the soil for the aforementioned reasons about how the decomposition of organic matter causes soil acidity.

Using Sulfur Based Fertilizers to Acidify the Soil

While most fruits and vegetables prefer to be grown in a neutral pH range (6-6.8), blueberries are unique since they prefer the pH of the soil to be in the more acidic range of 4.5 to 5.0. The soil pH is one of the most crucial factors that will determine if your blueberry bushes are healthy and productive, so it is important to adjust the soil pH to the proper levels before you even plant. Just like with the garden, it is absolutely imperative to test the pH of the soil in the intended area where you want to plant your blueberry bushes. For most soils, the pH will probably have to be lowered to more acidic levels. Remember, if you want to raise the soil pH to make it more neutral, you add lime to the soil. However, to lower the soil pH for blueberries, sulfur based fertilizers are one of the best options. What types of sulfur can be used and how does sulfur work in the soil?

The most common inorganic sources of fertilizers to acidify the soil are elemental sulfur, ammonium sulfate (preferred choice) and ferrous sulfate. Ferrous sulfate simultaneously acidifies the soil while supplying a rapid responding form of iron that should be readily available for the plant to utilize.[3] Often when plants which prefer acidic growing conditions are in a soil with a neutral soil pH, the plants will exhibit an interveinal yellow chlorosis, which is indicative of iron deficiency.[4] Even though there may be sufficient levels of iron in the soil, because the pH is not in the optimum range for acidic soil preferring plants, the plants will have difficulty acquiring and utilizing the iron in the soil. There are foliar sprays of iron which can immediately add iron to the leaves and improve the discoloration. However, this is only a temporary "fix", since the underlying problem, soil neutrality, is not being addressed. Luckily, the use of ferrous sulfate corrects both the iron deficiency in the leaves while fixing the source of the problem by acidifying the soil. Though ferrous sulfate is faster acting than the other types of sulfur, the only disadvantage of ferrous sulfate is that it is usually more expensive than other sulfur fertilizers. When I have blueberry plants with iron deficiency, I use both a foliar spray of iron plus I add some ferrous sulfate to the soil.

In addition, elemental sulfur acidifies the soil when the soil microbes oxidize each mol of sulfur, 2 mols of sulfuric acid are released into the soil.[3] The oxidation of sulfur via soil microbes and the subsequent release of sulfuric acid is the primary way the soil will become more acidic.[3] Though it takes more time to work in the soil, in the long run elemental sulfur is four to five times more powerful at acidifying the soil than ferrous sulfate.[3] Finally, ammonium sulfate is the top recommended fertilizer to use for blueberries since it supplies both nitrogen and sulfur to the soil. How much of these fertilizers should be used? Since this depends on multiple factors including soil type, this is why it is so important to take a soil test. After submitting it to an agency like a state agricultural extension office, this should provide a relatively exact amount. Here is an example of a general recommendation of how to fertilize by Oregon State University Extension Service:

- To lower the pH from 6.5 to 5.4 in a clay loam soil, apply 3.5 to 4.5 lb sulfur/100 sq ft.
- To lower the pH from 6.1 to 5.4 in a clay loam soil, apply 2 to 2.75 lb sulfur/100 sq ft.
- It is best to use the lower rate initially, check soil pH again in six months to a year, and apply more sulfur only if necessary. Do not apply more than 7 lb sulfur per 100 sq ft at one time.[4]

Notice how it is advised not to add too much sulfur at once but rather to do it progressively. Since you should be preparing the soil for a full year or two before planting blueberries, you can make multiple applications of sulfur to achieve the desired pH. Is there an optimum time of the year to add sulfur to the soil? According to the Oregon State Extension Service, fall applications of sulfur took about six months to acidify the soil.[4] Summer applications of sulfur took approximately three to four months to have their desired pH change.[4]

Furthermore, it is important to understand that when sulfur is applied to the soil surface, it takes a long time to move down the soil profile. Often, only the pH of the soil surface becomes more acidic while the root zone remains neutral. If you extract soil from the top layer and test the pH, it may indicate the pH is acidic enough for blueberries. However, the soil pH around the roots may be neutral which will adversely affect growth. For most efficient results when taking a soil test, make sure to collect soil a few inches down the soil profile. Luckily, there is an important method which can help distribute the sulfur throughout the soil more effectively than adding sulfur to the soil surface. If you intend to follow the additional pre-planting procedures like planting cover crops and perennial sod such as fescue in the growing area (explained in greater below), take advantage of when you are cultivating the soil by adding sulfur based fertilizer. Add sulfur to the soil surface and then use your equipment to cultivate the soil so the sulfur is more evenly mixed throughout the entire soil profile.

This method will help scatter the fertilizer throughout the soil and will help to lower more of the soil pH compared to if you just add sulfur to the top layer of soil. Remember, incorporating fertilizer into the soil reduces pollution of the atmosphere and the watershed. Simultaneously while adding sulfur, this is an excellent opportunity to correct nutrient levels in the soil by adding other fertilizers, especially bulk levels of phosphorous. During the year of application, only 10% to 15% of the phosphorus applied to the soil actually becomes available for the plants.[3] Since phosphorus availability tends to be low in most soils, one method to reduce the likelihood of phosphorous deficiency during the growing season, is to saturate the soil with high level of phosphorus fertilizer during the first few years.[3] Then, lower the rate of phosphorous to the recommended rate each year for the crop in order to reduce environmental pollution from an excess of phosphorus in the soil. This method should insure that since there are high levels of phosphorus in the soil, there will be sufficient levels available in a state that the plants can utilize as nutrients. If you are only planting a few bushes, then I would place sulfur and phosphorus fertilizers in the ground, cover them with a few inches of soil, and then plant the blueberry bushes.

Cover Crops and Sod

In addition to fertilizing the soil and adjusting the pH levels, planting cover crops and permanent sods like fescue and rye-grass is encouraged. This will enhance nutrient and organic matter levels in the soil, reduce weeds, and save time, money, and labor. If you are only planting a dozen or so blueberry bushes in the corner of your yard, making sure the soil pH is in the proper acidic range and planting a fescue and or rye-grass sod should be sufficient. However, if you intend to plant dozens of blueberry bushes in a large area, then using cover crops before planting blueberries is definitely advised. If you have a field and mow down the vegetation and then plant blueberries, it is likely that the area will be full of weeds. Over the years, you will struggle with trying to pick and spray all of the weeds, which will constantly keep growing around your blueberry bushes. I have seen firsthand on other farms and my own, how overwhelming weeds can be if you do not plant a cover crop followed by the establishment of a new sod before planting blueberries. Weeds like lambsquarters, crabgrass, and ragweed are not only a nuisance to remove, but while they are growing they compete with the blueberries for nutrients, air, water, and sunlight. Additionally, they can even spread diseases while also providing habitat and food for pests.

Moreover, if you rely on herbicides to control these weeds, it will become very expensive. If you continuously use the same herbicide with the same mode of action or active ingredient (herbicides with different names may have the same active ingredient), then some of the weeds may become herbicide resistant. Then as these weeds reproduce, you will have an infestation of herbicide resistant weeds, which will require the use of even more herbicides to control. Luckily, you can prevent yourself from having to over-rely on herbicides and their possible negative effects on the environment and your health if you take the time to plant cover crops and a new sod before planting your blueberries. When you use herbicides, insecticides, and or fungicides, make sure to vary the modes of action (active ingredient) so that the weeds, insects, and diseases do not become resistant.

In areas where cover crops and a fresh sod are planted, it almost seems magical how few weeds grow around the blueberry bushes compared to when these critical first steps are neglected! There are different cover crops to use specifically for blueberries including: buckwheat, Japanese millet, oats, annual and winter rye. When selecting cover crops for blueberries, remember you must choose ones which can tolerate more acidic pH levels. For most of these cover crops the intention is to use them as a "green manure". That means that at the ideal time (varies with each cover crop), the cover crops will be killed (mowed down or burned with an herbicide) and incorporated into the soil. After the cover crop is turned into the soil, to optimize growing conditions and reduce the time it takes to maintain the blueberries, establishing the growing area with specific grasses such as fescues and or perennial rye grass is recommended. An advantage of planting grass like fescue is that there are different varieties which grow slower than weeds and other types of grasses. Instead of having to mow in between the rows once a week, usually you only have to mow every two or three weeks!

Planting Time for Blueberries

Then after this sod is established, you can plant blueberries into this relatively weed free growing area. To do so, in the early spring about a week or two before planting, I use an herbicide to burn down the rows where I intend to plant the blueberries. Most herbicides will have information on the label which tells you how long to wait before planting. Usually this lasts a few days to a week. Just to make sure there is no herbicide residue left in the soil, I wait about a week to ten days before planting. If you do not want to use an herbicide you can lay black plastic down the rows where you intend to plant. By blocking out the sunlight, this method will also kill the vegetation. Either way, it is strongly advised to kill the vegetation in the rows before planting. If you do not kill the vegetation before planting, even if you add a thick layer of mulch, eventually the vegetation will grow through that mulch layer. Some people caution against using an herbicide at all the first year, but I have never had any problems with bushes dying from the herbicides. After your bushes are established, if you ever get herbicide on the bush, immediately cut off where the herbicide made contact and wash off the rest of the bush.

To further the suppression of weeds, I also sprinkle a pre-emergent granular based herbicide down the rows covered with a few inches of mulch. This pre-emergent herbicide will not harm existing growth, but rather will envelop weed seeds with a vapor preventing them from germinating. Some people suggest only adding two inches of mulch per year until you have a four to six inch layer of mulch. However, I have not noticed any difference between either method, so I add four to six inches the first year. As I am adding the mulch, I also sprinkle some pre-emergent herbicide into the mulch. Finally, I add a layer of pre-emergent herbicide to the top layer of mulch. This method is extremely effective at controlling weeds and saving you time and money. These pre-emergent granular herbicides usually work for about two to three months, so I re-apply them in mid to late summer. In addition to the granular form, there are spray forms of pre-emergent herbicide available.

In rows where there are four to six inches of mulch, in subsequent years only one to two inches of mulch will have to be added to compensate for the rate of decomposition. Applying pre-emergent granular herbicide before and after adding the mulch, combined with the mulch, should help to reduce the overall level of viable weed seeds in the soil. One of the principles of weed management is to reduce the total number of seeds in the soil by preventing growing weeds from going to seed, reducing tillage, and by killing weed seeds in the soil with pre-emergent herbicides.

What Should be Added to the Planting Hole?

In addition to cover crops, you can improve to organic matter levels in the soil by adding peat to the planting hole. The addition of peat helps to mimic the usual growing conditions of blueberries which are found in acidic soil high in organic matter. However, I usually only add enough peat so that it takes up no more than ¼ of the planting hole. It is advised to not fill up more than ¼ to ½ of the planting hole with peat. Especially important is to not add any synthetic fertilizer like sulfur to the planting hole since this can burn and potentially kill the roots (necrosis). Too many nutrients in the planting hole discourages the roots to grow.

Before filling up the hole, make sure to rake the sides of the hole, since when you dug out the hole, a hardpan probably formed along the outer edges. Every time you use a shovel or equipment to dig a hole, it is essential to break up the outer layer of the hole. If you do not break this hardpan, then the roots will have a difficult time growing outwards in all directions. Rather, they will grow in a circular manner because of the inability of the roots to break through the hardpan. As you fill in the planting hole with soil, at the halfway point, gently press down on the soil making sure there are no air pockets and add some water. While doing this, carefully move the blueberry bush in a circle. This insures there will be no air pockets and creates a sturdier soil, which is less likely to be disturbed especially if there are high winds. Next, continue adding soil until it is a little higher than the original soil level the blueberry bush was grown in. Then when you water, this should cause the soil to subside and the soil level will be at the original level the bush was grown in the pot. Once again, gently press down the soil to eliminate air pockets and to secure the bush.

The next step of adding mulch to your entire blueberry rows is one of the most important things. For educational and scientific purposes, I purposely neglected to mulch the second blueberry patch to see what happened. Sure enough, by mid-July some of these bushes were already dying and most of them were in a severe state of shock. However, the first blueberry patch did better since when I planted these bushes, I immediately mulched them. Even over a year later, the second patch is not as healthy and strong as the first patch.

Why is mulching so important? By blocking out direct sunlight from hitting the soil, the mulch helps to reduce water evaporation while simultaneously retaining water in the organic matter of the mulch. Furthermore, mulching helps to control weeds from growing and from competing for water, air, nutrients, and sunlight Mulching helps lower diseases and pests by reducing the amount of weeds. If there are no weeds growing around the blueberry bush, then it will dry off faster after it rains. This concept is important for all plants, since if the plant is constantly wet, this increases the risk for diseases. Also, if there are fewer weeds, there are fewer places for pests to hide. Then it will make monitoring and removing pests from your blueberry bushes easier.

Moreover, mulching adds valuable organic matter to the soil which improves soil structure, provides nutrients, and adds food and habitat for micro-organisms and earthworms. Remember these earthworms will help take organic matter from the soil surface into their underground networks. Then, they will eat it and release it as casts (poop) which will help fertilize the lower root zone. These underground networks help increase the water infiltration capacity of the soil while enabling the roots of the blueberry bush to expand more easily. Recall from previous chapters that the addition of certain types of organic matter to the soil increases soil acidity. After adding fertilizer, the addition of a mulch layer will help to prevent leaching of the fertilizer into the watershed and volatilization of the fertilizer into the atmosphere. Finally, when blueberry rows have a continuous mulch layer two to four feet wide going down the entire row, it makes mowing the grass easier. Instead of having to mow around each bush, you can just mow between the rows. If you follow these preliminary steps, then you too will be able to enjoy delicious and nutritious blueberries the year round.

How much sulfur based fertilizer should be used after planting? A general recommendation I adhere to after planting is as follows:

- For newly planted bushes in March or April, wait at least one month after planting and no later than the end of June, to apply 2 oz of ammonium sulfate per plant.
- It is best to divide the total number of oz needed each year and make two or three total applications a few weeks apart starting in March and finishing by the end of June.
- Avoid fertilizing after July 1st. Any new growth encouraged by the fertilizer will most likely not be strong and healthy enough to uphold itself against winter conditions which usually kill this unhardened and tender growth.
- For year two, add 3 oz ammonium sulfate per plant.
- Continue adding 1 oz per year until you reach 8 oz ammonium sulfate per plant.

How to Prune Blueberries

As with most fruits we plant, pruning at planting is important so the plant has a more equal shoot to root ratio. Often, 40% to 60% of the original plant should be pruned so that the plant has a greater chance of surviving. Now the roots can better establish themselves as they do not have to expend excess energy trying to feed a plant with too much vegetative growth. Therefore, I usually prune any branches greater than a foot tall back down to a foot tall. I also prune any smaller shoots and those growing laterally. For the first two to three years, it is recommended to remove any fruiting buds from the blueberry bush. The plant will establish a healthier root system and reach maturity quicker if it does not have to expend excess energy for fruit production.

For educational reasons, I did not prune fruit off some of the blueberry bushes I planted in the first few years. Sure enough, these bushes are smaller than the bushes which I pruned the fruit. While you may be eager to enjoy some fresh blueberries the first year or two, be wise and patient and remove the fruit buds before or immediately after they blossom. How do you know the difference between a fruit bud and a lead bud? Fruit buds are usually more round and thicker and are often located near the end of branches. Leaf buds are smaller, pointier and are located further down the branch. If you are unsure, allow the blueberry to go into flower and then remove the flowers since these will eventually become the fruit. The ideal situation is to prune fruit buds before blossom so that the plant will retain more of its nutrients compared to pruning after blossom.

For mature bushes, pruning is essential since it will increase yields and the size of the berry by allowing for more nutrients and sunlight to be available to these berries. Also, pruning enhances sunlight and wind infiltration which reduces diseases since the plant will dry off quicker after it gets wet. A well pruned bush allows for easier and more effective spray coverage since you have to use less spray to cover the bush. Pruning of older more established blueberry bushes revolves around the fact that generally after canes are six years old, their production begins to decrease. Therefore, I set up my pruning so it is on a constant cycle of pruning enough six year old growth that enough new growth is being established each year. This way you should constantly have new growth while having plenty of mature productive growth. To achieve this, I usually prune about 20% of the oldest canes which should allow for about five new canes to form at the base of the plant each year. The oldest canes usually have a grayish, flakey bark, more than an inch in diameter and can often be covered with lichens. To make pruning easier, first remove any obviously diseased or dead parts. Next, prune away any laterally growing canes which would otherwise get in the way while working and walking around the bushes. Also, try to prune the bush to allow for a more open canopy in the middle. Overall, pruned bushes have from ten to twenty young to old canes.

If you have an old, overgrown, and unproductive blueberry patch, one method to restore it is to cut all canes back to the ground level in early spring. About ten years ago when I first began growing food, I did this to the eight original blueberry bushes growing on the farm. However, I made the mistake of pruning them in fall which is not recommended since the pruning cuts can be damaged by the winter conditions. If you make this mistake just cover the cut bushes with a thick layer of leaves or straw to protect and insulate them. Luckily, they survived and now years later, these blueberry bushes are some of the most productive plants I have ever seen. I would also attribute restoring this patch to the combination of sulfur based fertilizers and the constant addition of mulch. After years of adding mulch, there is now 6 inches of dark and rich soil underneath the newly added top layer of mulch.

Protecting Your Blueberries

To prevent birds from eating the berries, you must protect them with netting or fencing. Otherwise, the birds will be the only ones to enjoy the fruits of your labor. Before I protected my bushes from the birds, I would literally only be able to eat a handful of berries a year. Again, when it comes to fencing and netting, you get what you pay for. While there are cheap blueberry nettings made specifically for birds, often the netting is so thin it breaks easily. Thus, make sure if you buy netting, that it is thicker and durable. Often bird netting comes in packages with ratios around 7 feet by 7 feet or 14 feet by 14 feet. These sizes are a nuisance since they barely cover any bushes and you have to use ties to connect them together. Luckily, I found 28 feet by 28 feet bird netting online which is much more efficient. One method is to simply drape the netting over the bushes. Another more convenient method which makes it easier to work/walk around the bushes and to harvest the berries is to build a frame and drape the netting over. Since I build a six foot wall around my berry patches to protect them from the deer, groundhogs, and rabbits, I overlap the netting with the fencing and tie it together. This forms a nice covered area which I can easily walk underneath. Make sure to fence to perimeter of the blueberry patch to prevent deer, groundhogs and rabbits from eating your plants. In the winter, rabbits and deer enjoy to eat the young tender branches since they are often one of the only food sources available for them.

Health Benefits of Blueberries

The color of the blueberry itself is indicative of high levels of anthocyanins. These are some of the most powerful anti-oxidants found in all of the classes of polyphenols, or the compounds which give fruits and vegetables their color.[5] As aforementioned, by destroying free radicals, which cause inflammation and destruction within the body's cells, anti-oxidants have been demonstrated to reduce the risk for cardiovascular disease, cancer, diabetes, and cognitive diseases like Alzheimer's. Specifically, according to Current Nutrition and Food Science Journal, "In vitro studies indicate that anthocyanins and other polyphenols in berries have a range of potential anti-cancer and heart disease properties…".[6] In fact, a study from Cancer Investigation concluded that anthocyanins demonstrated a greater ability to reduce tumor cells versus other flavonoids.[7] Though berries are much smaller than other fruits and vegetables, The Journal of Agricultural and Food Chemistry concluded that, "In general, blueberries are one of the richest sources of antioxidant phytonutrients of the fresh fruits and vegetables we have studied".[8]

Are you worried that there is so much new information in this book that you may forget it soon? Well luckily since you now grow blueberries and are a blueberry eating machine, improved cognitive performance is another one of the super health benefits of regular blueberry consumption.[9] For instance, The University of Cincinnati Psychiatry Department indicated that "…anthocyanins have been associated with increased neuronal signaling in brain centers, mediating memory function as well as improved glucose disposal, benefits that would be expected to mitigate neurodegeneration".[9] Once again, it appears the anti-inflammatory properties of anti-oxidants help to keep the brain healthy. Hold one for just a moment, I have to go eat a handful of berries!

How to Freeze Blueberries

Even though the composition of the nutrients in foods often changes depending on if and how they are cooked and how they are preserved, fortunately when blueberries are frozen, they still retain most of their original nutritional benefits.[5] This is wonderful news since the process of freezing blueberries is very easy and does not consume a great deal of time. After picking fresh berries, the first step is to wash the berries off and then remove any unwanted parts like stems and leaves. However, before you put the berries in the freezer there is a special trick which will prevent them from forming a solid frozen clump. First, allow the berries to dry after washing. Then, lay the berries flat on a cloth covered pan making sure the berries are not overcrowded and on top of one another. Next, put them in the freezer for a few hours up to a day. Finally, after they have frozen, you can then store the berries in various containers like mason jars. Now your berries will come out of the container individually like Skittles instead of being one solid clump. As a result, you can easily add a handful of berries to your diet throughout the entire year. Imagine how these little berries, in combination with the other healthy foods you now grow and consume regularly, are going to keep you happier and healthier.

How to Grow Raspberries

Raspberries (*Rubus*) are a relatively easy to grow and dependable perennial fruit which even in a small growing area, can produce substantial yields. Since they spread prolifically, you only have to start with a few raspberry plants. For red and yellow raspberries, plant about two feet apart and for black and purple raspberries, plant about three feet apart. Keep the spacing in between rows a distance of eight to ten feet. This may seem like a great deal of space at first, but as the raspberries grow, you will understand why this spacing is important. Adequate spacing will make it easier to work with, walk around and harvest the raspberries. Furthermore, spacing will allow plenty of sunlight and airflow to penetrate through the vegetation. Remember, providing sunlight and airflow is one of the most important concepts for growing food. The sunlight gives the fruit its color and combined with good air flow, will help dry the fruit and vegetation. This reduces the chances for common diseases of raspberries such as gray mold, spur blight, and anthracnose.[10] To further decrease the chance for diseases, avoid planting raspberries in excessively wet soils. Fortunately, to circumvent this problem, you can plant raspberries in raised beds.

In your raspberry patch the following year, you will have dozens and dozens of raspberry canes growing everywhere. By the spring, you will have so many new plants, that you can carefully dig up some of the canes and transplant them elsewhere so you can create a new raspberry patch. In fact, you will have plenty of canes for yourself that you will be looking for other people to share these canes. This is just another of the many ways that growing food can help you bond with family, friends, and neighbors. Each spring, I often give countless amounts of raspberry canes as gifts to different people so they can start their own raspberry patch. Then each year, these people will constantly think of you and thank you for giving them a gift that truly keeps on giving. However, perhaps the real reason I give them raspberry canes so they can is so that they stay out of my patch and I have more raspberries to eat for myself! Regardless, it is a win-win situation for everyone.

There are two major types of raspberries; "floricane-fruiting or summer bearing" which only produce fruit on two year old growth and "primocane fruiting or ever-bearing" which produce fruit on one year and two year growth. I prefer "ever-bearing" varieties since they produce fruit on one year growth and also bear fruit twice in one season. It seems from the end of June until November, these "ever-bearing" varieties constantly produce raspberries. After the end of year two, all growth will have to be cut back down to the ground level since fruit production stops by the third year. The optimum time to prune raspberries to ground level is between December and February. This is when the plant's nutrients have returned back underground to the crown of the plant. If you prune too early in the fall and too late in the spring, you will be removing valuable nutrients which will affect the vigor and health of the raspberries.

What are the nutrient and pH requirements of the soil? While blueberries favor acidic soil with a pH of about 4.5 to 5.0, and most fruits and vegetables prefer a more neutral soil of 6.0 to 6.8 pH, raspberries require a soil pH of 5.6 to 6.2. Just like the rest of the crops, make sure to plant in a sunny and well drained location. Immediately after planting, place about three inches of straw around the base of the raspberries since this will improve the likelihood of survival and increase growth. Once established, some say this straw should be removed since it has the potential to rot the base of the raspberries if they remain too moist. In my experiences I have not had any issues with using straw followed by the addition of woodchips. Of course if using high carbon mulches like wood chips, first add nitrogen fertilizer in order to prevent nitrogen immobilization. To fertilize raspberries using well rotted manure or compost, add a ¼ in layer to the soil and then mix this into the bulk of the soil profile before planting. Since raspberries do like a mildly acidic soil, I use ammonium sulfate fertilizer. I do not have an exact amount of how much should be used so I usually lightly sprinkle this into the soil before I plant. For already established plants, I lightly sprinkle some of this fertilizer around the plants in the beginning of the growing season. Then once the berries start to appear, I also lightly sprinkle some fertilizer around the plants. By adding a fresh layer of organic mulch each year with a small amount of ammonium sulfate fertilizer, my raspberry bushes thrive.

During the growing season, the most common pest problem I have encountered is with Japanese beetles. They can severely damage the vegetation and also transmit diseases through the process. To control them, I find that going around the plants once or twice a day and physically removing and killing the beetles is effective. You can drop the beetles into a container of soap and water or smoosh them in your hand like I do. Combined with the use of one or two applications of an insecticide/fungicide during the growing season, these methods are very effective. I often use the same sprays for my fruit trees on the raspberry bushes. I try to make sure to spray before there is edible fruit so I am not potentially contaminating the raspberries which I will eat. Before the early cropping in June, I make sure to spray. Then, after the first crop is over and before the second cropping occurs, I spray one more time. Furthermore, even before the growing season begins, just like with the other fruit I grow, I apply a petroleum based dormant oil spray to suffocate and kill any insect pest eggs. This spray is effective since it envelops insect eggs and prevents them from being born. Killing this first generation of pests is important to lower the risk of a pest infestation. Whenever I notice diseases, I will remove the entire cane before the disease can spread to the rest of the patch. So far this method has been extremely effective. Immediately after, make sure to disinfect your pruning tools before you cut another cane. These diseased canes should be discarded by burning or throwing away in the trash. Making sure your raspberries are planted in a well drained location will significantly reduce the amount of diseases.

Since raspberries can reach four to six feet tall and get loaded with berries, they might need to be supported. If you plant them along a fence line, you can simply run a thick wire down the row and tie it to the fence. Another option is to use the "T-Bar Trellis". Place a tall six foot post a foot into the ground. Then halfway up and at the top, place a horizontal piece of wood about two to three feet wide. Next, secure some thick gauge wire to the "T-Bar" and run it down the length of the row. Honestly, I have never tied my raspberry plants and have yet to encounter any problems. I simply prune the ones which are growing horizontal so the rows are more organized.

How to Freeze Raspberries

Freezing raspberries is the same process as blueberries. After picking the raspberries, place them on a flat, cloth-covered tray and put them in the freezer for a few hours to a day. Make sure the berries have adequate spacing and are not piled up on one another. Once again, this method allows for the berries to freeze individually so they come out of the storage container one at a time. To store them, I place them in glass mason jars in the freezer. My absolute favorite is to take the frozen berries and heat them up with some warm oatmeal, grass-fed butter and blueberries. They taste very similar to when you pick them fresh!

Health Benefits of Raspberries

Based on their rich red and darker purplish colors, right away it is evident that raspberries (like blueberries) are high in anthocyanins and contain all the aforementioned health benefits of this particular polyphenol. Furthermore, raspberries (along with strawberries, walnuts, and almonds) contain another polyphenol called ellagitannin.[11] Upon being ingested, the ellagitannins are transformed by microbes in our gut into ellagic acid and eventually into urolithins, which have been demonstrated to inhibit prostate and colon cancers.[11] Also, raspberries can help regulate blood sugar levels.[12] For instance, the synergistic effect of both anthocyanins and ellagitannins can help to control blood glucose levels after eating meals with high starch levels.[12] Another fascinating component of raspberries, is the ability of the polyphenol proanthocyanidin to reduce the absorption of fats from our diet, thus potentially helping to reduce the likelihood of obesity.[12] The ability of raspberries to regulate blood sugar levels while simultaneously reducing the absorption of fats seems to offer a delicious way to control/reduce the likelihood of diabetes and obesity!

In landscapes and yards all across the world, there is so much potential for people to plant blueberries and raspberries. These fruits are not only healthy and nutritious, but they will make your landscape and yard the talk of the neighborhood. Everyone will say your raspberries and blueberries are berry, berry good!

Chapter 6: How to Grow Fruit Trees

The preliminary procedures for planting fruit trees are alike to blueberries with one key exception. In most circumstances, instead of lowering the pH with sulfur based fertilizers, lime will be added to the soil to make sure the pH for fruit trees is in the neutral range of approximately 6.0 to 6.8. To grow fruit trees successfully, it is imperative to follow the aforementioned guidelines for proper site selection. For instance, to test and correct soil pH and nutrient levels, to plant cover crops and to once again establish as weed free of a growing area as possible by planting perennial grasses like rye and fescue.

Selecting a Rootstock

Luckily in our times, we have more cultivars of fruit trees and sizes to choose from than our ancestors. For most fruit trees, you can often select from three different sizes: standard (~25 feet), semi-dwarf (12 to 18 feet tall) and dwarf trees (5 to 12 feet tall). Now-a-days, we can determine how high the trees grow by selecting certain rootstocks which the fruit trees are grafted onto. For instance,

- the M27 rootstock (very dwarf) grows only 5 to 6 feet tall and should be planted 4 to 6 feet apart.
- M9 rootstock (dwarfing) grows 6 to 10 feet tall and should be planted 8 to 10 feet apart.
- M26 rootstock (dwarfing) grows 8 to 12 feet tall and should be planted 10 to 15 feet apart.
- MM106 rootstock (semi-dwarfing) grows 12 to 18 feet tall and should be planted 12 to 18 feet apart
- MM111 rootstock grows 20 to 28 feet tall and should be planted 18 to 24 feet apart.[1]

If space is limited, dwarf trees are a wonderful choice to plant in the landscape. If you see rhododendrons, other shrubs and small trees growing in a yard, then there is definitely room for dwarf-fruit trees. Even if you have a patio or a deck with room for an umbrella, then you can find room for a few potted dwarf trees. Amazingly, though they are smaller, dwarf trees produce a substantial amount of nice sized fruit. Since they do not grow as tall, dwarf trees are easier to maintain since you will not need a ladder to prune and to pick them. I have seen plenty of houses with small yards who were able to add a dozen or so dwarf trees. In fact, one of these houses gets an abundance of fruit from twenty trees that they even sell some fruit along the side of the road!

Adding fruit trees to your yard will increase the aesthetic beauty of the landscape. In the spring, fruit trees provide some of the most blissful flower blossoms in nature. As the season progresses, these flowers become colorful and vibrant fruits, adding flavor and life to the landscape. Friends, family, and neighbors will marvel at the sight of fruit in your landscape since most people have the same old boring yards. Though it seems like a simple notion to plant fruit around the house, they will think you are a genius! While they are foolishly competing over who has nicer grass, they will be astonished and jealous at how much more unique your property is once you plant some fruit trees. Even during the winter months, the snow covered fruit trees are an enjoyable sight.

In addition to their beauty, fruit trees increase the functionality of the landscape since you are providing yourself and the wildlife with food. A few years ago I planted a semi-dwarf tree in the flowerbed by the kitchen. One of the greatest joys in August and September is to walk a few barefoot steps outside the kitchen and to pick delicious apples right off the tree! Crunch, crunch, crunch! Breakfast, dinner and lunch! Moreover, there is satisfaction in knowing you are providing food for very important and species like bees. If you enjoy other types of wildlife like squirrels and chipmunks, they too will love to congregate around the fruit trees. So long as you plant enough of these trees, you should not have to worry about these critters from eating all of your fruit. However, if squirrels/critters become a problem, you can always set a cage trap and re-release them far away, or remove them in a manner which you please.

As we continue to build neighborhoods, towns, and cities, we have to remember we are simultaneously destroying habitat for animals and plants. Especially appalling, is the rapid construction of housing developments on old farmland. While I wish there would never be another development built on old farmland, that is not reality. So long as we consciously make an effort to plant beneficial plants like fruit trees in the landscape, then we can help mitigate the effects of development. Undoubtedly, from this point forward, we cannot continue to design and plant landscapes the way people have been doing for decades; with no regard for planting gardens, fruit trees, and native plants. The old way of caring about just having some grass in the yard must stop. The new way forward is to make sure we plant beneficial and beautiful plants like fruit trees in our yards, in addition to gardens of flowers, and vegetables.

These fruit trees can even improve the health and value of our lawns. For instance, they can provide shade for the grass and add nutrients to the soil. How do they do that? The tree itself will draw nutrients from deep in the soil and into the leaves and fruit. Then as these fall to the ground, they can add valuable organic matter and nutrients to the soil surface which otherwise would not occur if the fruit tree was not planted. Additionally, planting fruit trees can provide a beautiful and beneficial privacy barrier to the property. Consider how much more of a talking and selling point a house with fruit trees in the yard is compared to one that looks like every other yard.

Buying Fruit Trees

Where is the best place to buy fruit trees? Unfortunately, most local nurseries tend to sell fruit trees for around $30 to $75 dollars. To avoid such outrageous costs, I buy online and in bulk, so the fruit trees usually cost between $15 to $30 dollars. If you get your friends, families, or neighbors to place one large order, the price per tree and shipping cost drops. Whether you buy fruit trees online or from a nursery, an important requirement is that the fruit trees you buy are grown in an area that has a similar climate to you. For example, if you live in Maine, you do not want to buy fruit trees that are grown in Tennessee. Often, hardware and farm supply stores buy their fruit trees from warmer areas, so make sure to always check the original growing location. Why is this important? If you plant fruit trees which were grown in a warmer climate in an area where the winters are cold and snowy, it is more likely that this fruit tree will die. Therefore, I try to buy fruit trees from nurseries within my state and or climate. Luckily, with the internet, we have access to numerous choices of nurseries and trees. Also, if you want to plant fruit trees in the spring, make sure to place your order in the fall to make sure you get the varieties you want before they are sold out.

What type of trees should you buy? First and foremost, do your best to select trees which are disease resistant. For instance, apple cultivars like Enterprise, Goldrush, Liberty, Pristine and Redfree are resistant to apple scab, cedar apple rust, powdery mildew and fire blight.[2] Right away, selecting these resistant varieties will reduce the amount of sprays you will have to use while also lowering the amount of time and money it takes to maintain the trees. Furthermore, one of the guidelines to adhere to is to make sure you plant a few varieties of early, mid-season, and late fruit trees. Personally, I like to plant a minimum of three trees of each variety. Just in case one dies, you should still have plenty of fruit from the other two trees. When growing food, it is better to have enough for yourself and to share. If you only plant a few trees, you will be more likely to want to keep the fruit for yourself. However, if you plant a few of each variety, then you will probably have so much you will actually look for people to share the fruit. Most times, when you share food with people, they will return the favor and the flavor by making something delicious like a pie. On countless occasions, I have used fruit to barter for other goods and services. Additionally, when selecting fruit trees, you have to consider whether or not they are self-fertile or require other trees to cross pollinate.

What Time of Year Should Fruit Trees be Planted?

When is the best time to plant fruit trees? They can either be planted in late fall or late winter/early spring, preferably while the tree is still dormant and the ground is workable. When trees are planted dormant, they are more likely to survive since they have more time to adjust and to establish their roots. Therefore, since I am often busy in the fall, I prefer to plant fruit trees in the early spring. For experimental purposes, I also planted a few fruit trees during the summer months. With daily watering, they did indeed survive. However, they definitely grew less in the first few years compared to the trees which were planted while dormant.

Site Selection

Before you plant the trees make sure to check off the following list of aforementioned procedures. Does the planting site receive a minimum of six hours of direct sunlight a day in an area protected from excessive winds? Is the site far enough away from other trees? A safe guess is to visualize where the closest tree would land if it fell down. Make sure where you plant your fruit trees is far enough away from this drop zone. Is the soil pH in the proper range for the fruit you are planting which is preferably around 6 to 6.8 pH? Have you adjusted the nutrient levels in the soil? Concerning nutrients, be careful not to plant fruit trees in excessive rich soils or to over-fertilize with nitrogen, since this can cause too much vegetative growth and not enough fruit production.[1]

Furthermore, an important detail for planting fruit trees, especially in large quantities, is to select a site with a southern facing gentle slope of about 4% to 8%.[1] This will help the site warm up quicker in the spring and make it less susceptible to frost damage. Concerning frost, avoid planting your fruit trees in low lying areas since they are more susceptible to collecting cold air and frost. Additionally, is the planting site in a well-drained location so that water does not stay on the soil surface for long periods of time after it rains? During the dormant season it is okay if water drains less slowly than during the growing season. However, during the growing season, this can potentially kill the tree because of root rot and anaerobic conditions. According to *The Tree Fruit Production Guide* by Pennsylvania State University Extension:

> "Soil drainage is probably the most important factor in the longevity of an orchard. This is because of the inherent in-ability of certain types of fruit trees to survive when planted in imperfectly drained soils. Stone fruits (peaches, cherries, and plums) are the most susceptible to poor drainage. Apples are intermediate, and pears can survive on the more poorly drained soils".[1]

In one of my early orchards, I planted peach, plum, and pear trees in a location I thought had good soil drainage properties. However, I never checked the site in early spring. Sure enough, this area gets saturated with water during this time and numerous fruit trees have died. I learned my lesson and hopefully you do not have to make my mistake. So please make sure to plant your fruit trees in an area with good soil drainage properties.

Finally, have you done your best to remove the weeds from the planting site? Have you established a relatively weed free growing area by planting certain perennial grasses like rye and fescue? Specifically, many orchard growers recommend the use of Kentucky-31 tall fescue.[1] If you have sufficiently answered "yes" to these questions then I give you permission to plant some fruit trees! Remember, do not take shortcuts before planting thinking that you are saving time and money. It is much easier to correct pre-planting issues rather than trying to correct issues after you have planted the fruit trees.

If by the time you begin planting in early spring that the grass is already growing, I advise using an herbicide to kill the grass in the immediate area where you are planting fruit trees. Check the herbicide label to figure out how long you have to wait after spraying an herbicide to plant the fruit trees. Usually based on the herbicides I use, I am able to plant within a week after spraying. I have never had any problem with trees dying as a result of spraying an herbicide in the weeks before or after planting. However, some people suggest you should wait an entire year to use herbicides after planting perennial fruits. Why am I a proponent of using herbicides around fruit trees? Using herbicides around the base of a fruit tree helps that tree grow a few inches more per year compared to fruit trees where herbicides are not utilized. This makes sense considering that the tree now has less competition with grasses and weeds for water and nutrients. That top layer of grass and vegetation can take a significant amount of water (and nutrients) from being utilized by the tree. Thus, killing this vegetation allows more nutrients and water to be available for the tree.

How to Get the Fruit Tree in the Hole

When it is finally time to plant the tree, one of the most important things when digging the planting hole, is that before you fill the hole back in, make sure to break up the hardpan that has formed on the perimeter of the hole. Otherwise, when the tree roots grow and reach the hardpan, they will have a difficult time penetrating. Instead, the roots will often grow around in a circle which will severely reduce the trees productivity. I recently helped someone figure out what was wrong with their apple trees. After correcting the pH and nutrient levels, pruning and applying sprays, the tree was still not improving production. Then it dawned on me that perhaps they neglected this critical step of breaking up the hardpan and sure enough they were unaware of doing this. They also forgot to break up how the roots were growing around in a circle as a result of being grown in a pot. Before planting, make sure to gently break up the circular bound roots so that they are going out in all directions.

While planting the tree are there any soil amendments you should add to the planting hole? The answer to this question depends on who you talk. For instance, certain people warn against using any amendments in the planting hole since the fertilizers can burn the roots. Also, it is suggested that if the planting hole is too rich in nutrients, then the roots will grow more slowly. However, if there are no soil amendments added to the planting hole, this forces the roots to grow quicker in their attempt to find and utilize nutrients. What do I do? If I add fertilizer like bone-meal and blood-meal, both high in phosphorus, I will place it at the bottom of the planting hole and cover with a few inches of soil before placing the tree in the hole. If you decide you want to use fertilizer in the planting hole, just make sure it does not come into immediate contact with the roots.

If you are planting dry root trees, often some of the roots will be so long that you will have to cut them to make planting easier. For most dry root trees, I find that I have to make a few pruning cuts. One thing to pay attention to is to place the densest section of roots on the side of the planting hole facing the prevailing winds. This tends to be the direction from where the most consistent and strongest winds will blow. If you place the heaviest roots facing this direction, it should give the tree better anchorage which will reduce the chances the tree will fall down. Another trick I have used a few times is to place a heavy rock in the soil on the side of the prevailing winds. Of course after planting the tree, you can further secure it by staking the tree. If you intend to stake the tree, make sure to do it right away when you plant the tree so you are less likely to injure the roots.

While you are filling the planting hole back in, apply a similar method used for the blueberry bushes. To make sure there are no air pockets, by the time you fill half the hole in, add some water and wiggle the tree in a circular motion. As you are filling the hole, check that the graft union is at least two inches above the soil surface. Since planting holes often settle back in a few inches, I make sure this graft union is even up to four inches above the soil surface. Why is this important? If you plant this graft union in the soil, it will take root and now instead of having a semi-dwarf or dwarf tree, the tree will grow into a regular standard size tree. Moreover, if this graft union is planted in or too close to the soil, it is vulnerable to rotting faster and serves as an easier entry point for diseases and pests.

Once the soil is filled back in and is now flush with the surrounding soil, add more water and gently apply the same circular motion to the tree. Then, I add a fresh layer of soil which is actually a half inch or inch above the flush line. Why do I do this? Because after it rains, the planting hole will settle inwards a few inches. For the first few trees I planted, I neglected this step. As a result, the planting hole eventually settled so much that there was a depression where I planted the tree. Then too much water was collecting near these trees. Since the water weakened the soil, during heavy winds a few of the trees fell down. Furthermore, a few of the trees died of root rot. After realizing and admitting my mistake, I then had to re-plant the few surviving trees. Even while I was planting these first trees, I remember reading about making sure the tree was not planted in a depression. However, I shrugged it off and thought I could get away with it. From now on I am aware of the severity of improper planting. Thus, I always double check that at the end of planting my trees, the surrounding soil surface is actually a little bit above the flush line with the surrounding soil.

At planting time, it is recommended to prune 40% to 60% of the upper part of the tree so that the tree has a more equal shoot to root ratio. If you have too much vegetative growth and not enough roots, then it puts the tree in a stressful situation to try to feed the vegetation with limited roots. Especially during the first year and if there is a drought, this can shock and kill the tree. Unfortunately, I neglected to prune my first fruit trees after planting because I thought I could get away with it. However, after seeing how much healthier trees were if I pruned 40% to 60% of it at planting time, I now do this every time. It may seem like you are taking a few steps backwards, but in reality the tree will reach maturity quicker.

Why Remove the Fruit the First Few Years?

Another key trick to helping the tree grow faster is to remove the fruit for the first year or two after planting. This can be hard to do since obviously you want to enjoy fruit as soon as possible. However, in the long run, this will help the tree mature and reach full production more quickly. While I remove most of the fruit the first two years, I leave a few so I can enjoy the heavenly euphoria of eating a peach or apple just a year after planting. The easiest way to remove the fruit is to pick off the flowers or wait until after they blossom and tiny fruits begin to form. Do not wait until the fruits become large and then remove them since the tree has already invested valuable nutrients and energy into fruit production. The best thing is to immediately divert those nutrients and energy from fruit production into vegetative growth.

Fertilizing Fruit Trees

Concerning nutrients, how do you fertilize fruit trees after planting? When is the best time to apply fertilizer? Three to four weeks before the buds begin to get bigger in the spring is the best time to apply nitrogen based fertilizer.[3] According to Dr. Norman F. Childers of Rutgers University, "This gives the nitrogen ample time to be dissolved by rain, absorbed and transferred to the spurs and shoots, resulting in early development of large leaves, good shoot growth, good set of fruit, and rapid development in fruit size".[3] How should this fertilizer be added to the soil? To save money and the environment, instead of broadcasting the fertilizer over the soil surface, use localized placement of fertilizer.

For instance, from three feet away from the trunk to the area directly under the outermost branches I use a heavy metal bar to make a few holes about an inch or two across by about six inches to a foot deep. Make sure to avoid fertilizing within two to three feet of the trunk since there are often no or few feeder roots in this area.[3] Then, I add the fertilizer into these holes and cover them back with soil. Recall that only a tiny portion of a plant's roots have to come into contact with the fertilizer to acquire the fertilizer. By using localized placement, it saves money since you have to use less fertilizer because you do not have to add extra fertilizer to feed the grass. Moreover, since the fertilizer is placed in the ground and covered with soil, it reduces pollution since it is far less likely to be leached into the watershed and volatilized into the atmosphere. If you intend to broadcast fertilizer over the soil surface, then you will have to add enough fertilizer to make sure the grass is not stealing nutrients from the tree. For example, a mature tree with a 40 foot spread will require an additional pound of nitrogen fertilizer to feed the grass.[3]

How much fertilizer should be used? While a foliar analysis of your trees will give you a much more precise amount of nitrogen (ammonium nitrate) fertilizer needed, a general way to make an estimate is to measure the trunk diameter in inches and divide this number by three.[3] That total number would be the amount of nitrogen fertilizer in pounds to add to the tree. What is a foliar analysis? According to Dr. Crassweller of Pennsylvania State University:

"Foliar analysis is the process whereby leaves from fruit trees are dried, ground, and chemically analyzed for their nutrient content. Nitrogen, phosphorus, potassium, calcium, magnesium, iron, copper, boron, and manganese are among the elements tested for. A foliar analysis can help determine what fertilizer(s) a grower needs to apply. Unlike soil tests, which only show what is in the ground, a leaf analysis shows what the trees actually absorbed. Soil tests do not typically give accurate measurements of nitrogen or the minor elements".[4]

How do you collect a foliar analysis? Dr. Crassweller explains that the best time to collect leaves is from mid-July to mid-August since this is when nutrients are most stable within the tree.[4] Otherwise, in the beginning and end of the season, the nutrients are constantly moving throughout the tree.[4] How many leaves should you collect? Dr. Crassweller recommends taking 60 to 70 leaves from different trees of the same cultivar (variety), being careful not to mix leaves of different cultivars and of younger and older trees.[4] Also, it is advised to collect leaves from the middle section of this year's growth.[4] To keep up to date on the nutritional values and requirements of your fruit trees, the foliar analysis should be performed every three years.[4] In between the testing, one of the ways to observe if you fruit trees have adequate nutrition is to measure how many inches of new growth has occurred in the last year. For instance, for mature trees you want at least a minimum of six inches but preferably up to fourteen inches of new growth per year.[3] Younger non-bearing trees should have fifteen to thirty inches of new growth per year.[3]

What about the use of manure as fertilizer? To get the same amount of nitrogen from manure versus chemical fertilizer, you would have to use 20x the amount of manure.[3] For this reason, I mainly use chemical fertilizer for my fruit trees. Luckily, if your trees are big enough that they do not have to be fenced off to protect them from the deer, the deer themselves will add plenty of manure to the orchard. Is deer manure enough to fertilizer the trees? For about twenty years, the original apple orchard at the farm was neither pruned nor intentionally fertilized. Even after I began to prune them, I did not add chemical fertilizer for a few years. It was only after I began to use chemical fertilizer that the trees began to produce larger and healthier apples. Additionally, trees that did not bear fruit began to once again produce fruit after a few years of adding chemical fertilizer. Therefore, based on these observations, I noticed that the combination of chemical fertilizer with the natural addition of deer manure results in better fruit. Since the use of chemical fertilizer helped non-bearing trees to produce once again, now more deer will visit these trees to eat the apples and will simultaneously excrete manure. One of the ways I restored the unproductive mature trees was by following the recommendation to apply double and even quadruple the fertilizer for a few years or until production and vigor is obviously restored. Then once this occurs, reduce to fertilizer to the recommended rate per year.

Pruning Apple Trees

An art form in and of itself, pruning apple trees will enhance their aesthetic beauty and make the trees more productive. Some of the most significant advantages of pruning are that it will decrease the amount of leaves, branches, and fruit that the tree needs to supply with nutrients. Therefore, more nutrients will be available helping to improve fruit production by increasing the size and quality of the remaining fruit. The ideal time to prune is in late winter and early spring before the tree becomes active. Under the best circumstances, you want to finish pruning before the buds of the trees begin to swell. When the buds swell in early spring, this is an indicator that the tree is now actively growing. If you prune an actively growing tree, you are removing valuable nutrients. However, if you prune during the dormant season, most of these nutrients are being stored by the tree in the root system. Also, it is easier to prune trees when there are no vegetation, insects, and bees. It is advised to finish pruning by the time the tree blossoms. However, you can prune the trees up to the middle of the summer. The key point to remember is to give the pruning cuts enough time to heal by the winter. Avoid pruning in the fall since the pruning cuts will be susceptible to winter injury caused by severe cold temperatures, ice, and snow.

Pruning will enhance the health and vigor of the trees for a variety of reasons. For example, pruning increases the ability of sunlight and air to infiltrate the tree. This combination will help the tree dry faster which is important to reduce the risk of diseases. Increased sunlight will help the fruit develop fuller color and increase its market value. Furthermore, a well pruned tree will result in more optimum spray coverage, reduce the amount of sprays you have to use, and will lower the amount of time it takes to spray the trees. However, it is important to prune trees in stages. Otherwise, if you prune too much of one tree in one year, it can kill the tree. Therefore, a general rule is to only prune 1/3 of the tree per year.

How exactly do you prune an apple tree? First, I walk up to each tree facing the same position each time (6'o clock for me). Then, I work counter-clockwise and focus on one section at a time, instead of being overwhelmed and worrying about the entire tree at once. The first pruning cuts to make are to remove any diseased or dead branches. If you remove a diseased section of a tree, cut it off a few inches away from the diseased part. Afterwards, immediately sanitize and disinfect your pruning tools or else the dirty tools can spread diseases. Furthermore, after cleanup, burn or discard the infected and or dead wood since this can harbor pathogens which can potentially infect healthy trees. Next, remove any branches which are growing into one another both vertically and horizontally. Try to keep at least a foot of space between the canopy of the tree. Finally, remove the watersprouts or "suckers", the non-fruiting branches which grow straight up. Some people say to cut the suckers first. However, you can save yourself time and labor if you first remove the dead, then overcrowding horizontal and vertical branches. Often, these branches have suckers, so you are accomplishing two things at once. The ideal shape for a mature standard apple tree is that it looks like an umbrella with the branches extending outwards preferably at a 45 degree angle.

Health Benefits of Apples

Is the English adage, "an apple a day keeps the doctor away" really based on scientific fact? The numerous phytochemicals (biologically active compounds in plants like carotenoids, flavonoids, and phenolic acids which give them their color, flavor and smell) found in apples, such as catechin, chlorogenic acid, phloridzin, and quercetin, all have powerful anti-oxidative properties, which have been demonstrated to reduce the risk of asthma, cancer, cardiovascular disease and diabetes.[5] Various studies conducted over decades, involving more than 100,000 participants from multiple nations, indicated that a higher consumption of apples was associated with a reduced risk of lung cancer.[5] Specifically, this has been suggested to be a result of the flavonoid quercetin (also found in onions) and the flavonoid catechin (also found in tea).[5] Interestingly, these studies indicated that consuming onions and or tea alone did not show a reduction in the risk for cancer, cardio-vascular and or cerebrovascular diseases.[5] Rather, it was only when apples were part of the diet that a reduction in diseases was evident.[5] Besides reducing lung cancer, apples have also been demonstrated to lower the risk of asthma.[5]

In addition to reducing the risk for cancer, a seven year study of 40,000 women indicated those with the highest amount of flavonoids (responsible for the yellow color of fruits and vegetables) in their diet were 35% less likely to have cardio-vascular diseases.[5] Concerning cerebrovascular diseases (stroke, or anything which reduces normal blood flow in the brain), a Finnish study concluded that people who consumed the most apples were the least likely to experience a stroke.[5] Regarding diabetes, the high level of quercetin found in apples has been demonstrated to lower the risk of type II diabetes.[5]

Obviously, the adage "an apple a day keeps the doctor a day" is based on science. Therefore, planting apple trees will not only increase the aesthetic beauty of your property but will improve your health by lowering the risk for cancer, cardiovascular, cerebrovascular, asthma, and diabetes. It is remarkable how an apple which can fit in the palm of your hand can have such profound health benefits.

How to Grow Peach Trees

The site requirements for peaches (*Prunus persica*) are very similar to apples except with the following rule. With peaches you must be careful to plant them in a very well drained location since of all the fruit trees, they are the most susceptible to dying if they are planted in a poorly drained location. Less tolerant of colder winter conditions, peaches should not be planted in areas where winter temperatures reach -10°F.[1] Selecting trees which are certified to be either or both virus-free budwood and virus-free rootstock will reduce detrimental diseases like Prunus stem pitting.[1] When choosing peach trees, decide if you want clingstone, which the flesh of the fruit adheres to the pit, or freestone which the pit easily falls off the fruit. Once again, pick a few varieties of early, mid, and late season trees to insure a continued harvest throughout the season. Whenever I am selecting trees I have never grown before, I find asking neighbors, local growers, or talking to the supplier is helpful since these people can offer suggestions at what grows successfully in the area.

When it comes time to physically plant the peach tree, adhere to the same aforementioned guidelines for planting apple trees. When you are ready for the tree to go into fruit production, peaches should be thinned to about six to ten inches apart on the branches. Though there are chemical sprays for other fruits like apples to lower the number of blossoms on the tree, peaches are mostly thinned with the hand. Instead of using a ruler, I just spread my thumb and pinky out and leave about that much space in between the peaches. You must thin the peaches or the weight and numbers of the peaches will cause the branches to fall over and break. Also, thinning will improve the quality of the remaining fruit on the tree.

Pruning Peach Trees

Just like with the other fruit we plant, 40% to 60% of the original peach tree should be pruned at planting. At this time, try to keep branches which have a nice 45 degree angle since when they mature will be less likely to break and will produce the most fruit. How do you to train peach trees? There are two common methods. One method I often see on commercial farms is when the peach tree has two main limbs at about a 45 degree angle, which look like a V. The other option is to have three to five limbs growing off to the sides at a 45 degree angle, leaving the center of the tree open. Remember to avoid pruning in the fall or winter since this can cause winter injury to the peach tree. I often begin pruning my peach trees in February while the tree is dormant. Preferably, I try to prune everything before the buds begin to swell and the tree breaks dormancy. Once again in the summer, prune some of this year's vegetative growth a few weeks before the peaches ripen. This increases air circulation and allows the sunlight to enhance the color and quality of the fruit. Luckily, since peach trees grow prolifically, if you make pruning mistakes, by next year, there will be enough new vegetative growth you will be able to correct your mistakes.

Spraying Peach Trees

Of all the different types of crops I grow, it is impossible to successfully grow peaches without the use of sprays to control both insects and fungal diseases. The first five peach trees I planted died in the second year from peach leaf curl. To control this devastating disease, after about 90% of the leaves have dropped in autumn, spraying a copper based fungicide spray is essential. In the spring while the tree is still dormant, this copper based spray should be applied again. Concerning peach leaf curl, it is imperative to spray before you see the symptoms during the growing season. Though some say that there is nothing you can do to get rid of peach tree curl during the growing season, this past year by removing and disposing the affected leaves and spraying a copper based spray, the peach leaf curl went away. Make sure to dispose of the infected leaves properly by burning them or throwing them away in the garbage. While it is not always advised to use copper based sprays during the growing season, I did it regardless. I just reduced the recommended rate.

Just like with controlling diseases in other plants, the use of sulfur based sprays is recommended to control diseases during the growing season. The point of the sulfur based sprays is not to cure the disease once it starts, but to prevent it from forming in the first place. These growing season sprays should be used once the trees break dormancy in the spring. Should you spray while the peach tree is in blossom? Some people say spraying while a fruit tree is in blossom should be avoided to prevent potential damage to bees. Other people say it is imperative to spray during blossom to prevent the early stages of the diseases from occurring. Depending on the weather, sulfur based sprays are used more frequent if the weather is rainy and less frequent is the weather is dry. If there is wet weather predicted in the forecast, make sure to spray beforehand, since the wet weather serves as an optimum time for fungal diseases to spread. Remember, the goal is to spray to prevent the diseases from occurring in the first place. Ideally you want at least 24 hours of dry weather after spraying to the sprays have time to be absorbed by the tree.

To control insects, using petroleum based dormant oil spray after leaf drop in the fall and in the later/winter early spring when temperatures are around 40 degrees Fahrenheit is imperative. The oil works by coating the eggs of overwintering pests. This prevents oxygen from entering which suffocates the insects before they can even hatch. Dormant oil spray is important since it prevents the first generation of insects from being born and reproducing. Before pest infestation levels are reached, it is wiser to take a proactive approach and prevent the levels from rising in the first place. One thing I learned is that you need to wait about two weeks to a month between applications of your dormant oil spray and copper/sulfur based spray. As always, whenever using sprays make sure to read and follow all directions.

During the growing season, using sprays like Captain and Malathion will help to prevent and control insects and diseases. Make sure to read the label and see how long you have to wait after spraying to harvest and eat the peaches. I usually do not spray my peaches for about a month before harvest, just to make sure I am reducing my exposure to potentially harmful chemicals. If you want to enjoy peaches then you must spray. Otherwise, the insects and diseases will destroy the tree and fruit leaving you with nothing but a headache and yearning for some fresh tree ripened peaches. To naturally decrease the amount of pests which harm your plants, the addition of beneficial insects like Anthocorid bugs, Earwigs, Lacewings, Lady beetles, and Hoverfly larvae to the growing area can lessen the need for insecticides.[6] Finally, removing and discarding rotting fruit, fruit that has fallen, diseased/dead branches, peach pits on the tree or in the ground, and removing fallen leaves from the growing area will reduce diseases and pests. The combination of chemical, physical and biological control are effective measures to lessen diseases and pests while improving production.

Health Benefits of Peaches

According to the International Society for Horticultural Science, red flesh peaches have equal or greater antioxidant effects than blueberries, prevent the estrogen-receptor negative MDA-MB-435 breast cancer cells from growing and are effective at reducing the oxidation of low-density lipoprotein or bad cholesterol.[7] The carotenoids lutein and zeazanthin (cause orange, red, and yellow colors) in peaches have been demonstrated to lower to risk for developing eye cataracts, or a filmy clouding of the eyes which negatively affects vision.[8] Moreover, the lutein in peaches lowers the risk for another eye ailment, macular degeneration, or a buildup of fatty deposits under the retina which causes blurry or loss or vision.[9] These two carotenoids in addition to beta-carotene (precursor to Vitamin A), have been demonstrated to reduce the risk for lung cancer.[10] Researchers at Texas A&M University revealed that peaches contain the following major phenolic acids: anthocyanins, chlorogenic acids, quercetin derivatives and catechins, which work together to produce anti-obesity, anti-inflammatory and anti-diabetic properties.[11] While different companies are trying to come up with supplements which isolate these anti-oxidants and pack them in high doses in pill form, it seems nature knows and works best. For instance, these anti-oxidants are most effective when they are consumed as a whole peach.[11] Peaches are another food you can grow yourself which has the ability to lower your risk for diseases caused by excess oxidation and inflammation such as cancer, heart disease, diabetes, obesity, and eye ailments like macular degeneration and cataracts. The next time you eat a peach, hopefully one you grew yourself, as you bite it and the juices get all over your hands and run down your face, think of how nutritious and healthy this delicious fruit is for you! May you forever grow healthy and happy!

References

Introduction

1.) Park, Bum Jin, et al. "The Physiological Effects of Shinrin-yoku (Taking in the Forest Atmosphere or Forest Bathing): Evidence from Field Experiments in 24 Forests Across Japan." *Environmental Health and Preventive Medicine* 15.1 (2010): 18-26.

2.) Sisson, Mark. *The Primal Connection.* Primal Blueprint Publishing, 2013.

3.) Ramagopalan, Sreeram V., et al. "A ChIP-seq Defined Genome-wide Map of Vitamin D Receptor Binding: Associations with Disease and Evolution." *Genome Research* 20 (October 2010): 1352-1360.

4.) Cotman, Carl W. and Nicole C. Berchtold. "Exercise: A Behavioral Intervention to Enhance Brain Health and Plasticity." *Trends in Neurosciences* 25.6 (2002): 295-301.

5.) Visser, Susanna N. et al. "Trends in the Parent-Report of Health Care Provider-Diagnosed and Medicated Attention-Deficit/Hyperactivity Disorder: United States, 2003–2011" *Journal of the American Academy of Child & Adolescent Psychiatry* , Volume 53 , Issue 1 , 34 - 46.e2

6.) Coley, David, Mark Howard, and Michael Winter. "Local Food, Food Miles and Carbon Emissions: A Comparison of Farm Shop and Mass Distribution Approaches." *Food Policy* 34.2 (2009): 150-155.

7.) Lipinski, B. et al. 2013. "Reducing Food Loss and Waste." Working Paper, Installment 2 of Creating a Sustainable Food Future. Washington, DC: World Resources Institute. (June 2013)<worldresourcesreport.org>. Accessed 21 November 2017.

Chapter One

1.) Joy, A., and Hudelson, B. (2010, May 7)."Black Walnut Toxicity." *University of Wisconsin Horticulture.* <hort.uwex.edu/articles/black-walnut-toxicity> Accessed 29 May.2017.

2.) Haas, Brian J., et al. "Genome Sequence and Analysis of the Irish Potato Famine Pathogen Phytophthora Infestans." *Nature* 461.7262 (2009): 393-398.

3.) Brandle, Jim, and Laurie Hodges. "Windbreaks for Fruit and Vegetable Crops." *National Agroforestry Center*. University of Nebraska, 2012. <nac.unl.edu/documents/morepublications/ec1779.pdf>. Accessed 3 Mar. 2017.

4.) Anten, N. P. R., Alcalá-Herrera, R., Schieving, F. and Onoda, Y. (2010)."Wind and Mechanical Stimuli Differentially Affect Leaf Traits in *Plantago major.*" *New Phytologist*, 188: 554–564. doi:10.1111/j.1469-8137.2010.03379.x

5.) Brown, James KM, and Mogens S. Hovmøller. "Aerial Dispersal of Pathogens on the Global and Continental Scales and its Impact on Plant Disease." *Science* 297.5581 (2002): 537-541.

6.) Brady, Nyle C., and Ray R. Weil. *Elements of the Nature and Properties of Soils*. 3rd ed. Upper Saddle River: Prentice Hall, 2010. Print.

7.) Pears, Pauline, ed. *Rodale's Illustrated Encyclopedia of Organic Gardening*. 1st ed. New York: DK Publishing, 2002. Print.

8.) Cloern, James E. "Our Evolving Conceptual Model of the Coastal Eutrophication Problem." *Marine Ecology Progress Series* 210 (2001): 223-253.

9.) Bricker, Suzanne B., et al. *National Estuarine Eutrophication Assessment: Effects of Nutrient Enrichment in the Nation's Estuaries*. US National Oceanographic and Atmospheric Administration, National Ocean Service, Special Projects Office and the National Center for Coastal Ocean Science, 1999.

10.) Magdoff, Fred, and Harold Van Es. *Building Soils for Better Crops. Sustainable Soil Management*. 3rd ed. Brentwood: Sustainable Agriculture Research and Education Program (SARE), 2009. Print.

11.) "Soil Quality Indicators: Aggregate Stability." USDA Natural Resources Conservation Service, Apr. 1996. <www.nrcs.usda.gov/Internet/FSE_DOCUMENTS/nrcs142p2_052820.pdf>. Accessed 3 Mar. 2017.

Chapter Two

1.) Brady, Nyle C., and Ray R. Weil. *Elements of the Nature and Properties of Soils*. 3rd ed. Upper Saddle River: Prentice Hall, 2010. Print.

2.) "Inherent Factors Affecting Soil Organic Matter." *Natural Resource Conservation Service*, United States Department of Agriculture, <www.nrcs.usda.gov/Internet/FSE_DOCUMENTS/nrcs142p2_053264.pdf.> Accessed 21 May. 2017

3.) "Municipal Solid Waste Generation, Recycling and Disposal in the United States: Facts and Figures for 2012." United States Environmental Protection Agency, Feb. 2014. <www.epa.gov/sites/production/files/2015-09/documents/2012_msw_fs.pdf>. Accessed 23 May. 2017

4.) Favoino, Enzo, and Dominic Hogg. "The Potential Role of Compost in Reducing Greenhouse Gases." *Waste Management & Research* 26.1 (2008): 61-69.

5.) Childers, Norman F. *Modern Fruit Science*. 8th ed., New Brunswick , NJ, Rutgers University, 1978. Print

Chapter Three

1.) Gleason, Mark Lawrence, and Brooke Aurora Edmunds. *Tomato Diseases and Disorders*. Iowa State University, University Extension, 2005.

2.) Brady, Nyle C., and Ray R. Weil. *Elements of the Nature and Properties of Soils*. 3rd ed. Upper Saddle River: Prentice Hall, 2010. Print.

Chapter Four

1.) Sanchez, E.S., P.A. Ferritti, and Et Al. *Vegetable Gardening. Recommendations for Home Gardeners in Pennsylvania*. State College: Penn State University. 2 July 2010. <extension.psu.edu/plants/vegetable-fruit/production-guides/vegetable-gardening-1/Vegetable-Gardening.pdf>. Accessed 26 May. 2017

2.) Griffiths, Gareth, et al. "Onions—A Global Benefit to Health." *Phytotherapy Research* 16.7 (2002): 603-615.

3.) Manach, Claudine, et al. "Polyphenols: Food Sources and Bioavailability." *The American Journal of Clinical Nutrition* 79.5 (2004): 727-747.

4.) "Antioxidants: Beyond the Hype." *Harvard School of Public Health*.<hsph.harvard.edu/nutritionsource/antioxidants/>. Accessed 29 June. 2018

5.) Lü, Jian-Ming et al. "Chemical and Molecular Mechanisms of Antioxidants: Experimental Approaches and Model Systems." *Journal of Cellular and Molecular Medicine* 14.4 (2010): 840–860. PMC.

6.) Hertog, Michael GL, et al. "Dietary Antioxidant Flavonoids and Risk of Coronary Heart Disease: the Zutphen Elderly Study." *The Lancet* 342.8878 (1993): 1007-1011.

7.) Smith, Bruce D. *The Emergence of Agriculture*. New York: Scientific American Library, 1995. Print.

8.) Weaver, Connie, and Elizabeth T. Marr. "White Vegetables: A Forgotten Source of Nutrients: Purdue Roundtable Executive Summary." *Advances in Nutrition: An International Review Journal* 4.3 (2013): 318S-326S.

9.) Doubrava, Nancy, and Powel Smith. "Broccoli." *Home & Garden Information Center | Clemson University*, South Carolina, Clemson University Cooperative Extension Service, Apr. 2003. <hgic.clemson.edu/factsheet/broccoli/>. Accessed 4 July. 2018.

10.) U. Thapa, P. H. Prasad & R. Rai (2016) Studies on Growth, Yield and Quality of Broccoli (Brassica Oleracea L.Var Italica Plenck) as Influenced by Boron and Molybdenum, *Journal of Plant Nutrition*, 39:2, 261-267, DOI: 10.1080/01904167.2014.992538.

11.) Angeloni, Cristina, et al. "Modulation of Phase II Enzymes by Sulforaphane: Implications for its Cardioprotective Potential." *Journal of Agricultural and Food Chemistry* 57.12 (2009): 5615-5622.

12.) Zhang, Yuesheng, et al. "Anticarcinogenic Activities of Sulforaphane and Structurally Related Synthetic Norbornyl Isothiocyanates." *Proceedings of the National Academy of Sciences* 91.8 (1994): 3147-3150.

13.) Dufault, Robert J, and Marjan Kluepfel. "Tomato." *Home & Garden Information Center | Clemson University*, South Carolina, Clemson University Cooperative Extension Service, 26 June 2012. <hgic.clemson.edu/factsheet/tomato/>. Accessed 8 July. 2018

14.) Bhowmik, Debjit, et al. "Tomato-a Natural Medicine and its Health Benefits." *Journal of Pharmacognosy and Phytochemistry* 1.1 (2012): 33-43.

15.) Giovannucci, Edward. "Tomatoes, Tomato-Based Products, Lycopene, and Cancer: Review of the Epidemiologic Literature." *Journal of the National Cancer Institute* 91.4 (1999): 317-331.

16.) Anderson, Richard A., et al. "Elevated Intakes of Supplemental Chromium Improve Glucose and Insulin Variables in Individuals with Type 2 Diabetes." *Diabetes* 46.11 (1997): 1786-1791.

17.) Devore, Elizabeth E., et al. "Dietary Antioxidants and Long-Term Risk of Dementia." *Archives of Neurology* 67.7 (2010): 819-825.

18.) Currais, Antonio, et al. "Modulation of p25 and Inflammatory Pathways by Fisetin Maintains Cognitive Function in Alzheimer's Disease Transgenic Mice." *Aging Cell* 13.2 (2014): 379-390.

19.) Adhami, Vaqar Mustafa, et al. "Dietary Flavonoid Fisetin: A Novel Dual Inhibitor of PI3K/Akt and mTOR for Prostate Cancer Management." *Biochemical Pharmacology* 84.10 (2012): 1277-1281.

Chapter Five

1.) Demchak, Kathleen, et al. "*The Mid-Atlantic Berry Guide for Commercial Growers*, 2013-2014." Pennsylvania State University College of Agricultural Science (2013).

2.) de Silva, Amal, et al. "Phytophthora Root Rot of Blueberry Increases with Frequency of Flooding." *HortScience* 34.4 (1999): 693-695.

3.) Brady, Nyle C., and Ray R. Weil. *Elements of the Nature and Properties of Soils*. 3rd ed. Upper Saddle River: Prentice Hall, 2010. Print.

4.) Hart, John Mervyn, et al. Nutrient Management for Blueberries in Oregon. *Oregon State University*, 2006.

5.) Lohachoompol, Virachnee, George Srzednicki, and John Craske. "The Change of Total Anthocyanins in Blueberries and Their Antioxidant Effect After Drying and Freezing." *BioMed Research International* 2004.5 (2004): 248-252.

6.) Beattie, Julie, Alan Crozier, and Garry G. Duthie. "Potential Health Benefits of Berries." *Current Nutrition & Food Science* 1.1 (2005): 71-86.

7.) Kamei, Hideo, et al. "Suppression of Tumor Cell Growth by Anthocyanins in Vitro." *Cancer Investigation* 13.6 (1995): 590-594.

8.) Heinonen, I. Marina, Anne S. Meyer, and Edwin N. Frankel. "Antioxidant Activity of Berry Phenolics on Human Low-density Lipoprotein and Liposome Oxidation." Journal of Agricultural and Food Chemistry 46.10 (1998): 4107-4112.

9.) Krikorian, Robert, et al. "Blueberry Supplementation Improves Memory in Older Adults." *Journal of Agricultural and Food Chemistry* 58.7 (2010): 3996-4000.

10.) Hanson, Eric, et al. "High Tunnel and Open Field Production of Floricane-and Primocane-fruiting Raspberry Cultivars." *HortTechnology* 21.4 (2011): 412-418.

11.) Landete, J. M. "Ellagitannins, Ellagic Acid and Their Derived Metabolites: A Review About Source, Metabolism, Functions and Health." *Food Research International* 44.5 (2011): 1150-1160.

12.) Mcdougall, Gordon J., and Derek Stewart. "The Inhibitory Effects of Berry Polyphenols on Digestive Enzymes." *Biofactors* 23.4 (2005): 189-195.

Chapter Six

1.) Halbrendt, J.M. et al. *Tree Fruit Production Guide.* The Pennsylvania State University, 2013.

2.) Hofer, Marie. "Low-Maintenace Apple Trees." <HGTV hgtv.com/outdoors/flowers-and-plants/trees-and-shrubs/low-maintenance-apple-trees>. Accessed 21 Aug. 2017.

3.) Childers, Norman F. *Modern Fruit Science.* 8th ed., New Brunswick , NJ, Rutgers University, 1978. Print

4.) Crassweller, Robert M, et al. "Peach Production." *Penn State Extension*, Penn State University. <extension.psu.edu/peach-production>. Accessed 14 Aug. 2017.

5.) Boyer, Jeanelle, and Rui Hai Liu. "Apple Phytochemicals and Their Health Benefits." *Nutrition Journal* 3.1 (2004): 5.

6.) Pears, Pauline, ed. *Rodale's Illustrated Encyclopedia of Organic Gardening.* 1st ed. New York: DK Publishing, 2002. Print.

7.) Byrne, D. H., et al. "Health Benefits of Peach, Nectarine and Plums." II *International Symposium on Human Health Effects of Fruits and Vegetables*: FAVHEALTH 2007 841. 2007.

8.) Vu, Hien TV, et al. "Lutein and Zeaxanthin and the Risk of Cataract: the Melbourne Visual Impairment Project." *Investigative Ophthalmology & Visual Science* 47.9 (2006): 3783-3786.

9.) Olmedilla, B., et al. "Lutein in Patients with Cataracts and Age-Related Macular Degeneration: A Long-Term Supplementation Study." *Journal of the Science of Food and Agriculture* 81.9 (2001): 904-909.

10.) Mayne, S. Taylor. "Beta-Carotene, Carotenoids, and Disease Prevention in Humans." *The FASEB Journal* 10.7 (1996): 690-701.

11.) Texas A&M AgriLife Communications. "Peaches, Plums, Nectarines Give Obesity, Diabetes Slim Chance." ScienceDaily. 18 June. 2012. <sciencedaily.com/releases/2012/06/120618132921.>. Accessed 22 Aug. 2018.

To Keep Updated On What is "Growing" On

www.farmerpat.net

YouTube – Farmer Pat. Back To Your Roots

Instagram – farmer_pat_youtube

Facebook – Farmer Pat @produceyourproduce

Gmail – farmerpat240@gmail.com

Feel Free To Contact Me

Made in the USA
Lexington, KY
21 December 2019